CREEP THIS WAY

HOW TO BECOME A HORROR WRITER

WITH 24 TIPS TO GET YOU GHOULING

Written by Rebecca Cuthbert

"...Cannot be recommended enough. It's a breath of fresh air..."
— Joshua Gage, *Cemetery Dance Online*

Pitched and edited by Christopher Ryan

Published by Seamus and Nunzio Productions, LLC

Book Cover by Rebecca Cuthbert and Jensen Sikora

First edition 2024

ISBN: 978-1-7325355-6-5

PRAISE FOR CREEP THIS WAY

"The good, the bad, and the remainder. In an age where authors cling to withered laurels, or outright overrepresent their qualifications, I consider *Creep This Way* to be one of the most necessary additions to the collection of any writer who wants to save time! It is not a dime-a-dozen book for learning how to write in the Horror genre. The author of this book receives my deep respect because she is brave enough to acknowledge all the mistakes it took to become the fantastic writer she is. Each step and misstep is courageously recorded and balanced with the equally valuable knowledge acquired."

–Moaner T. Lawrence, author, "The Great American Nightmare"

"Rebecca Cuthbert brings us a how-to-write book for any level of expertise and a roadmap for navigating all the extra pieces that go with being a writer these days. Creep This Way offers you 24 tips to not only understand writing, but social media, website design, the importance of live events, writing groups, how to build confidence, and how to embrace the inevitability of rejection. In an industry that is constantly changing, even seasoned pros will learn something new from this book."

–James Sabata, author, *Caduceus*, *Fat Camp*, and *The Cassowary*

"Rebecca Cuthbert is an inspiration, both for her talent and tenacity. Her practical and accessible advice in Creep This Way is honest, and at times hilarious, with just the right amount of macabre analogies. If you've ever longed to explore horror in any form but felt too shy, intimidated, or looked-down-upon, this book is absolutely for you!"

-Lindsay Merbaum, author, *The Gold Persimmon*; founder and mixologist, Pick Your Potions

"Cuthbert's "how-to" is a delightful blend of memoir and no-nonsense advice for all aspiring writers. Framed within her heartwarming brand of optimism and you-can-do-it attitude, it reads like an older sister offering up her sage advice."

-Rowan Hill, author, *Foxfire*

"*Creep This Way: How to Become a Horror Writer* by Rebecca Cuthbert is a fun yet insightful how-to book that differs from other instructional guides in a very important way: it doesn't teach you how to write. While other handbooks focus on the nuts and bolts of writing, such as dialogue, plot, setting, etc., Cuthbert has done something no one else has, created a book for beginners that is all about the 'everything else' that goes with being a writer. Things like how to find writers' groups, how to behave on social media, how to manage your time. There are even chapters on how to dress, how to get over rejection, and how to avoid scams targeting writers. All of it written in an easy, entertaining style filled with personal anecdotes detailing her own path from starting out to becoming a published author. Creep This Way: How to Become a Horror Writer is a must-read for anyone thinking about dipping their toes into the writing pool, whether it be horror or any other genre."

– JG Faherty, Horror Writers Association Mentorship Program Manager; author, *Ragman*, *Songs in the Key of Death*, and *The Wakening*

"Dripping in big sister energy, Cuthbert lays out an easy-to-execute guide for any new writer. I wish I had this three years ago."

-Roxie Voorhees, author, *The Longest Thirst*

"Brevity may be the soul of wit, but Cuthbert proves it's also perfect for delivering education and inspiration! In just a handful of pages, the advice in *Creep This Way* alternates between motivational and practical, giving authors crucial tools for a writing career. A must-read!"

-Christopher O'Halloran, editor, *Howls From The Wreckage*

"*Creep This Way* is an essential guide for the aspiring horror writer. Rebecca delivers sound advice—with warmth, wit and charm—sure to kickstart your career. What are you waiting for? It's time to join the 'Halloween people!'"

-D.M. Guay, author, *24/7 Demon Mart* book series

"Rebecca Cuthbert verifies her triple threat qualifications as an author by offering *Creep This Way* for those interested in gaining insights into writing in toto. The text, while horror centric, contains so much useful information and insight that anyone wanting to write as an avocation or vocation will walk away from the book enlightened in some way. The tone is conversationally didactic, which makes the book super engaging and a joy to work with. For writers, this is the how-to text you've long sought. For teachers, this text will be a godsend for classes in genre writing or writing in general. Rebecca Cuthbert knocks it out of the park; clearly a five-star piece for writers of all levels and 9-college faculty."

-Rocky Colavito, author, *Creative Control* and the Neo-Giallo Series

"*Creep This Way* is packed with incredibly valuable advice for first-time authors and masters of the craft alike. From habits and tips to research, this is a great grimoire on how to jump in and do it all at once. It proves that honing your craft is more than the work you put out. It's also the relationships you build, and how you can pay it all forward."

–Sofia Ajram, author, *Coup De Grâce*

This book is dedicated to all the new and established horror writers who answered the door when I knocked.

-Rebecca Cuthbert

What she said.

-Christopher Ryan

"You never know what you are going to want until you see it clearly."

-Shirley Jackson, *The Haunting of Hill House*

"I love when a plan comes together."

-Col. John "Hannibal" Smith, *The A-Team*

Contents

FOREWORD

I published this book because I wanted to read it. And I want to learn from it. Repeatedly.

I have read a hell of a lot of books on the topic of writing and becoming a professional author (see *For Further Study*), but I've never been able to find a really approachable gateway book, a first volume "how to do this" kind of guide about both writing and fundamental aspects of the business.

And then I met Rebecca.

Here is someone whose voice stands out in every social media post, story, and poem because there's an honesty, humility, and approachability about her, a friendliness that confirms she's one of us.

She is also a go-getter, someone who is unafraid to try. And I believe that is the key to real world publishing success.

Some people say you need an "in," a godfather or godmother or godperson, someone who will guide you past the gatekeepers. Good on you if you have that. Most of us don't.

Others insist that you need astounding, undeniable talent, and of course that helps too. Most of us don't have that either.

What most of us who are reading this forward in this book right now do have is passion. We are called to tell stories. Why else would we be reading this page?

And we may have experience writing stories (and if you need more information on that, we'll show you where to go), but the truth is, there's more to storytelling than just pounding the keyboard. We need to know what to do after the inspiration. I believe that Rebecca Cuthbert is the perfect person to offer exactly that information. She's straightforward and honest and she is one of us.

Additionally, she's researched where to submit her stories and poems once she's written them. This mystifies so many of us. Rebecca's got our back.

She has also faced the fears and doubts we all have, and she offers tips on how to overcome them.

Equally important, she's gotten into the habit of pushing "send" without freaking out, and often enough, has gotten published. In this book she discusses how to develop good habits in this area as well.

She's also forced herself to attend public events, met people in the industry, and summoned the courage to say hello. If you have any hesitation on those fronts, Rebecca has solid advice for you.

Lastly, she's figured out the social media of it all without losing her soul. Her chapters on those topics are not to be missed.

Bottom line, Rebecca Cuthbert is going to teach you what you've been hoping to learn. How do I know? Because she taught me with this book. I learned a lot.

Now, you.

OK, Rebecca will take it from here.

Christopher Ryan
editor, publisher
Seamus and Nunzio Productions, LLC

MAKE A START

My identity as a writer has wavered over the years, fading and reappearing like a struggling but determined ghost.

During my undergrad years, I was overconfident about my writing skills. Attending the MFA program at West Virginia University in my late 20s showed me all I didn't know. And while that was wonderful and necessary, the program was all about *literary fiction*, full of writers who wanted to be the next Raymond Carver or Flannery O'Connor. And then there was me, sitting at the table with a bright smile and bangs that I tried to make work, all like, "Hey! I like ghost stories!"

It's not like I was an outcast. I made friends there that I still have. I learned a ton. But, I muffled that part of me until "I like ghost stories" was a whisper only I could hear; in those workshops, "genre" was a bad word and no "serious writer" would admit to liking it. I remember clearly that in one special-guest-leader workshop, Randall Kenan (RIP) got to my story–about a dog who was maybe a reincarnation of a dead dog and maybe not–and said, "Well. I don't know what to say about this one!" and that was that from him. No notes. No pointers. I wanted to curl into a ball under the table and cry, not because he disliked my work (that would have been fair; art is subjective), but because he wouldn't even consider it. He didn't even see it as a legitimate story worthy of discussion. (Pro Tip: Never be *that writer*.)

After three years of teaching and writing and workshopping, I graduated and got married to Joel, my longtime partner. I took a job as an adjunct professor in 2012, teaching creative writing at the college where my dad used to work as a security officer–SUNY Fredonia. I published a few "literary" pieces here and there in the subsequent years, even getting into, with help, *Brevity*, a well-respected flash nonfiction journal published by Ohio University. No part of me even whispered about ghost stories anymore. It had been drilled into my head by the culture at WVU: Literary fiction good. Genre fiction bad.

What a crock of shit.

In 2020, during the Covid-19 pandemic lockdown, I went through a bit of a metamorphosis. I did not go from caterpillar to butterfly, and I didn't wake up to find I suddenly had the body of a cockroach. What I did was turn from a self-doubting "literary" writer into a genre fiction writer of the badass bitch variety. And I haven't looked back.

(Shoutout here to Lisa Kröger and Melanie R. Anderson, who published *Monster, She Wrote: The Women Who Pioneered Horror & Speculative Fiction* with Quirk Books. Reading it was like a slow infusion of courage and inspiration: the women featured wrote spooky stories by candlelight, in torturous dresses with boning and bustles, sometimes keeping all of it secret from disapproving husbands. But me? The only serious obstacle I faced was a lack of confidence, and that was fixable. More on that later.)

Thus, my genre-writing self was miraculously revived. That voice came back–*my* voice, it was *always* mine–and it came back screaming: "I LOVE GHOST STORIES!"

In the three years since, my life has changed in ways I wouldn't have believed even if I had a crystal ball. And I know you're not me–you've got your own life with your own opportunities and challenges–but I hope you'll read on to see how I earned my way into the horror genre and, more importantly, joined the horror writing community. The steps and methods I offer you are customizable, and you can go at your own pace. With every chapter, you'll see that if this socially-awkward, ghost-loving weirdo could be embraced by The Halloween People (Credit: Kevin Wetmore), then so can you.

That's my backstory...

Now, you.

Grab a notebook, laptop, or whatever you write on, and answer these for yourself. This is your part of this book, and, hopefully, these questions and recommendations will become significant steps in your journey to fulfill your writing dreams. Ready? Let's go.

What are your favorite horror subgenres?

What do you want to write?

Whose words do you feel inspired by?

And now the tough one: What's been holding you back? What's the worst that could happen if you gave yourself an hour, sat down at your desk or kitchen table, took out your notebook and wrote: *The last place I'd want to spend the night alone is...*

...and then what if you kept going?

Try it. I dare you.

Okay, I double dare you.

Get Back to Learning

Once I knew what I wanted–to be a writer, to develop a voice, to publish more than occasionally–I went about planning how to get it (this is the cool stuff you came here for). And know what I realized? I needed HELP.

I still had my buddies from grad school, and, like my own in the spring of 2020, their dance cards were empty. When summer rolled around, the five of us–me, Kelly Sundberg, Heather Frese-Sanchez, Keema Waterfield, and Sara Lucas–formed an "official" online writing group. We sent each other work, scheduled meetings (and happy hours), and provided feedback for one another on stories, poems, and essays.

For those who have never been part of a writing group or workshop group, I highly recommend them. Sometimes these are run more formally–like through a graduate or undergraduate program; sometimes more casually–like through a local library or community center; and sometimes they are totally friendly and no-pressure–like a few friends getting together. All of these can be in person or online. In any form, the writers involved will trade stories/poems/whatever, give each other feedback, and meet to discuss revision possibilities. If done right, workshops inspire you to write more, to revise again, to keep going. It's important to find one or start one that is right for you. (*More on that in Chapter 16—Consider a Writing Group.*)

And damn, did trading feedback over those summer months feel good! Because though I'd led dozens and dozens of undergraduate creative writing workshops over the last eight years, I hadn't been part of a structured peer workshop since grad school.

Wonderful as the experience was, though, it didn't satisfy me for long. Like a vampire with grade-A arterial blood, getting a taste only made me want more: more experience, more skill-building, more knowledge, more discussion. The hunger for improvement was heady as a curse. If I didn't give into it, I would shrivel up until my skin was tissue-thin and my fingernails fell off.

So, using Google, EventBrite, Facebook, and Twitter (now, um, X), I found online learning opportunities, like classes and workshops, author talks and craft presentations. Some of these had moderate price tags attached, others were super inexpensive or even free.

Look for classes and workshops that are targeted toward your genre(s) and needs. The search words and phrases I usually try are "horror," "horror writing," "horror writing workshop," "ghost stories," "gothic," "speculative writing class," "horror readings," etc. Joining and attending these events will help you improve your writing skills, provide you with more in-depth knowledge about your genre, and give you examples of what the best-of-the-best horror writers are out there publishing.

One of the first resources I jumped on was an independent study with Lindsay Merbaum, an author of speculative fiction (*The Gold Persimmon*) and for-real-deal witch. I signed up for Feminist Horror in early 2021 and got hooked. Next it was Queer Magical Realism, and then Witches, and then... Well I've kind of lost count, because I've taken every single independent study Lindsay has offered since then, and not only do I adore her, but the rest of our Study Coven is pretty kick-ass too. (Interested? Visit www.pick-your-potions.com.)

Around the same time, I contacted a friend and fellow writer, West Moss, who was then offering developmental editing and "story doctor" services. I paid (reasonable fees–we'll talk about affordability a little later, I promise) to work with her on a few of my stories, all speculative, with elements spanning the subgenres of horror, weird, magical realism, and more. And wow, did those stories improve. Some of them I'd just written, and some were dusted off from my grad school days. With her, I came to understand that I wasn't working on a random array of stories. I was working on a curated story collection, a melange that could be called "literary speculative" or "elevated horror" or whatever other label you like for stories that blend literary fiction with genre fiction.

It was a shock to discover what I suspect you will discover about yourself by the end of this book: I had a thing, a WIP (work-in-progress) just like all the "real" writers who I followed on social media. I had a goal and a focus, and *Six O'Clock House & Other Strange Tales*, a manuscript made up of 13 stories, came into the world. (I'm still shopping that one around with publishers; cross your fingers for me!)

Many of the stories, poems, and essays started in the classes and workshops of '21 and '22 (both those included in *Six O'Clock House & Other Strange Tales* and independent pieces) have found homes (*see Chapter 11—Do the Research, Part 2: Submissions*). "Still Love," a poem first drafted during my Feminist Horror class, was published by *Nocturne Horror Magazine* and eventually earned both a Pushcart Prize nomination and a Best of the Net nomination. It's also in my debut poetry collection, *In Memory of Exoskeletons* (more on that later). Another piece from Feminist Horror, a flash fiction story called "Punching In," earned a finalist spot in Crystal Lake Entertainment's Shallow Waters flash fiction contest for the "time fuckery" theme in 2023. "Punching In" is also part of my LitSpec story collection. Another story, "Falling to Pieces," written during Queer Magical Realism, was published first in *Defunkt Magazine* and then again in Neon Hemlock Press's *We're Here: Best Queer Speculative Fiction of 2022*. The poem "Lake Erie Omen," first drafted in a *Defunkt Magazine* Lit Fest "monster" workshop, was published in the summer '23 issue of *Sirens Call E-Zine*.

I'm not trying to brag (much). What I want to show you is evidence that learning to invest time and effort in myself, and in my craft, eventually paid off. These classes and workshops taught me how to write better and more widely; suddenly I wrote poems and stories in genres I hadn't even considered before.

Now, you.

First, make sure you're following other writers and publishers/presses on social media and on platforms like Substack and Patreon. Look up your favorite authors; follow them and then look at the list of accounts they follow. Keep doing this–soon you will have a huge list of awesome people and publishers to inspire you. Keep an eye on all of their posts; this can often help you find classes and workshop opportunities. Sign up for your favorite authors' newsletters and follow their blogs. Check out EventBrite for online activities–talks, panels, and Q&A sessions–and remember to use genre-specific keywords that will give you results you want.

If you find later that you've followed so many accounts that it becomes overwhelming, that's an easy fix; just stay with the ones that have been helpful or inspirational and unfollow those that either aren't helpful or contribute to the overwhelm. You can always check them out again in the future.

As great as online opportunities are, don't forget to look closer to home. Does your local library or continuing education center offer anything interesting? Are there any author readings or meet-n-greets scheduled at your local bookstore? Find an event and attend it. Be open to what you can learn, not just from the teacher/leader but from fellow students and attendees, as well. And if there's nothing shaking when you want it to be, head over to YouTube and subscribe to writers' videos and tutorials. Here are a few: Writer Brandon McNulty, *The Indy Authors Podcast*, *Buzz Book Expo*, *Outstanding Screenplay*s, *Galactic Terrors*, *This is Horror*, and (gotta mention the editor's show!) *Tell The Damn Story*.

Pro Tip: Writing is an artform; there's always room for personal growth and new ideas! If Stephen King had stopped learning and experimenting after *The Shining*, we never would have gotten *It*! Noodle on that.

Set Up an Author Website

Let's talk about author websites.

You may be thinking, "I'm just getting started. Why would I create a website?"

Because an author website is like a vial of holy water. You want to have it *before* you need it.

Creating an author website is important for a few reasons. I'll go over them, and then explain how to get started.

The first reason you should have a website is that it's a place you design and arrange to showcase yourself. You get to control the first impression you make on everyone who searches you online. That's a pretty powerful tool.

Another reason to create an author site is to be searchable in the first place. You don't want potential readers to Google you only to find same-name strangers on hundred-year-old census reports and scammy address-and-phone-number sites. And if you think you can rely on social media accounts alone for an online presence, think again: some people aren't on social media at all, and those who do have accounts may not use the same platforms as you. (After all, there's a new platform every week!)

If people can easily find you online, they can also easily contact you. Setting up a contact page on your website means you can receive messages from folks via webmail form; you don't have to post your private email address. (How to do that comes a little later, I promise.)

When I decided to create my author website in 2021, I had to face the fact that I am a tech idiot. I don't know how to use my television's remote control. Sometimes I can't even find the power switch on a computer. So, I hired my friend Amanda Dedie, who is a freelance website guru, to design a simple site for me. (Fun fact: Amanda is the person who, years ago, explained to me what a hashtag is so I could be #cool too.) We chose the website hosting company WordPress, because it lets me update my website easily, and its basic subscription level was within my budget (there's even a free option). Amanda and I talked about color schemes, design, and necessary pages in advance, with me telling her, "I want basically like a haunted library vibe." And that's what she gave me. (See her work at www.rebeccacuthbert.com.)

You might be wondering what the heck to put on a website when you're just starting out. I did, too.

I will admit here that I needed to dig pretty deep for website content at first. If you're in the same boat, don't worry, you'll find content; I did. I had a smattering of creative publications to list (and link) on a "Publications," page, as well as an interview or two to list on a page I called "Press." Then there were lifestyles articles and book reviews from my freelance days, organized onto pages called–you guessed it–"Articles" and "Book Reviews." Those journalism-type publications were far from horror focused (like, I wrote one about jam), but hey, posting them was a start. (I didn't have a "me" back then to give me pointers, but you have me, and I have suggestions for you. Don't panic.)

Amanda also added "About" and "Contact" pages to my site, but it still looked skimpy. So, I decided to start a new blog, accessible through my website, called "Writer's Block & the Ticking Clock." I keep it active, though I don't adhere to a regular posting schedule. There, readers can find not only my musings on writing, but interviews with other authors and guest posts from writers I admire. (I see the blog more like a community corkboard than a podium–*see Chapter Five—Find Your Tribe*.)

I paid Amanda for the design and creation, I paid for a WordPress subscription, and I paid for a domain name: rebeccacuthbert.com. But if your budget doesn't allow for those expenses, you still have options.

For example, WordPress, as well as other web content management systems, offers free subscription plans (some do not, but offer free trial periods; make sure you read the fine print). If you go a no-cost route, your website won't be too flashy, and your design templates will be limited–but you will still have a place where people can find you and learn more about you. And, should things go well, you can always upgrade later to a paid plan. Plus, many aspects of your website are more important than flashiness (I get to that below), all of them achievable with free or low-cost website subscription plans.

For example, your website should be clean and clear and easy to navigate. Give your pages simple and obvious titles; no one will know that "Personal Radness" is your biographical "About" page. And if you mention other sites or authors or their books, always include hyperlinks to make them "clickable."

By the way: to hyperlink, highlight a word on your webpage, like "Goodreads," then click the icon that looks like a chain. You will get an empty text box; copy the URL (https://www.goodreads.com/) into it and hit "Enter." Voila! Now folks can click on it and be taken to Goodreads, or wherever you'd like to send them. Hyperlinks make me feel like a powerful wizard!

Back to website design. Go with a solid background color instead of a trippy pattern for all your pages, and make sure your text fonts are easy to read–Times New Roman, Calibri, and Georgia are always smart choices, and font should be 12-point size for page material and 14-point or larger for titles and headings. Stay away from Comic Sans (no one likes that one), and anything that looks like cursive or calligraphy (sorry, Freestyle Script and Harlow Solid Italic).

Do not add animated graphics. They're obnoxious and can mess with people's eyes and give them headaches. When you create a new page, give it a clear label; these will appear across your homepage. These could be "About," "Published Work," "Contact," etc. (Don't make people scroll down to find things!) Add social media icons to your homepage that link to those accounts so people can follow and friend you. (Some subscriptions give you these in an options list; if not, copy and paste an icon from any Google Image search, then link it the same way you'd add a hyperlink–see above.)

If you don't have a ton of content initially, don't worry–you have enough to start with. Include an "About" page with a short biography and a photo–this can be a nice selfie; it doesn't have to be a professional portrait. Add a "Contact" page that leads to a webmail form for the reasons listed above (Wordpress allows this through its "Contact Form to Email" plugin via its "Plugin" menu; then just fill in your information).

And definitely start a blog or a newsletter about a writing-related topic and give it its own page! As I said above, I run mine as a community space–I always want it to be a platform through which I can boost my friends, help them announce their projects, and gather their thoughts for more rounded information in articles. But your blog could be about novel-to-movie adaptations you love (and don't), book reviews, music playlists you create for different story collections, favorite podcast episode recommendations, or something else. Post and publish whatever represents you–though it's probably a good idea to stay clear of politics, religion, personal romantic entanglements, grudges, hatespeak, and how mad you are that Pumpkin Spice Lattes only come around once a year.

(Actually, maybe *do* write about that last one–you'd probably get some traction there.)

When it comes to how much or how often to post, publish blog or newsletter updates on whatever schedule works best for you, but keep at it. Audiences for these things build up over time. (You can link a Patreon or Substack account to your website if you already have those accounts established. A friend of mine even uses his Substack account in place of a website, because it does what he needs it to–gives him a platform and makes him searchable online.)

An unexpected advantage of creating my author website was seeing how much I *had* done–I'd never looked at all my achievements in one place before, and realizing I had an entire body of work made me proud of myself. When the website was ready to go live, it gave me a boost of confidence. It was another one of those little milestones: I got to say "I have an author website." I added it to my email signature and my social media bios–more proof that I was, in fact, a "real" writer.

My website has changed quite a bit since 2021. Yours will, too, as you grow into your writing *and* your writing life. As I accrued publications in multiple categories, I divided them into separate pages: "Fiction," "Nonfiction," and "Poetry." (You can also organize by genre, like "Horror" and "Sci-Fi" and "Fantasy.") But that gave me too many pages–my website looked cluttered with all those tabs. So, I deleted my "Articles" and "Book Reviews" pages, since those publications no longer felt relevant to my life. I also deleted my "Contact" page in favor of an icon on the homepage, to save room–Amanda set that up using the same "Contact Form to Email" plugin.

Soon enough, my "Press" page had to become "Media," since I had more to mention than an old interview or two–I'd won awards, earned honors, placed in writing competitions, and gotten mentioned in articles. (My first book was reviewed by Joshua Gage in *Cemetery Dance Online*–a fact that still has me floating.) My book has its own page. I had to add "Podcasts," as I have both been a podcast guest (invited by hosts) and had my fiction and nonfiction read on podcasts (*see Chapter 11—Do the Research, Part 2: Submissions*). These days, I'm updating my website every other week. (If you do pay someone to create your website, make sure they teach you how to update it! You don't want to rely on someone else for every little change.)

Now, you.

Stop thinking you're not worth a website.

Once you're over that, establish a budget and stick to it. Whether you're DIY-ing it or hiring someone, research not only website management companies, but also designs you like. Look at your favorite authors' websites. What are the styles? What's included? How are they organized? Is navigating those sites intuitive?

If you hire someone, make sure you check out other sites they've built and confirm that you like their work first. Get a timeline from them, and ask what they need from you. Plan to meet, in person or via Zoom or Skype, throughout the process. Have them teach you how to do basic updating and corrections.

If you build your own author website, watch all the tutorials you can and read how-to articles. It's worth a shot to see if your local library or continuing education center offers help with web design. And remember how you need to be looking for learning opportunities? See if you can find a free or low-cost website design workshop, in person or online.

Other important stuff:

-Have a friend proofread your site before you make it live. Spelling errors, misused homophones, and incorrect punctuation will make you look unprofessional.

-Don't pirate material. Use pictures from free sites, like freepik.com, which only requires you to cite a picture's source. Use your own photos, or use licensed photos from a gallery site you subscribe to. The last thing you want is to get in trouble because you used a picture for which you didn't have rights.

-Graphic design sites like Canva have free account options. The templates and available photos will be limited, but you'll still find the design tools useful, not only for website material but for social media posts. (*For more on social media, see Chapter Twelve.*)

Dress the Part

This chapter isn't about changing who you are or hiding the magic that makes you *you*.

It's about representing yourself to the people in your new community–at cons, readings, festivals–in ways that help them get to know you better, and that establish you as a professional in your genre. Don't worry; the range of what works for different writers is wide open! The key is to be your authentic self.

As for me, I am not goth. I'm not punk. I'm not a skater or a metalhead. And I won't wear clothing that would feel like a costume just to fit in. If I did, I'd look as awkward as I'd feel. But in the horror world, there's room for everyone–even gals like me, who wear an awful lot of beige.

Yes, I consider "oatmeal" to be its own worthy and specific color.

At cons, I dress up a little. I wear my well-fitting jeans instead of my frumpy-schlumpy jeans. I put on a structured blazer over a Poe t-shirt instead of a baggy cardigan. If there's an awards dinner or if I'm doing a reading, I'll wear a skirt or dress–vintage looking, if I have it. (Most of my wardrobe is from thrift stores and clearance racks, by the way. I'm cheap and proud of it.)

Why should you bother? Because adding a little polish will boost your confidence and show that you're taking yourself seriously as not just a writer, but an author–dress for the job you want, you know? Additionally, putting some effort into your appearance shows organizers (and the living horror legends in attendance) that you care about the con itself, and that you're excited to be there.

But it's not just about dressing up–it's about turning out. Advertise your fandoms so that your people can find you. Wear your *Hellraiser* hoodie, your Stephen King hat, your Medusa earrings. Bring your bag with all the pins and patches. Those little bits of flair (*Office Space* reference intentional) are conversation starters and will help you make new friends.

If you want to get wild, though, get wild! Where else is it more appropriate to do so? I've seen people at cons in full Victorian dress, in steampunk tophats, and in leather masks. I've spoken to folks in chain mail and mesh shirts, and attended readings with people in rainbow onesies and thigh-high boots. If it makes you feel good and it showcases your personality, go for it! Just remember that strong looks are polarizing–they'll pull some folks to you and ward off others.

Also, ask yourself what function you are fulfilling there: are you attending as a fan or an author? Sometimes what we wear as fans doesn't represent who we are as authors.

However, don't let thinking about your appearance become a burden. How you dress is likely something you've already considered as part of your own identity, even if you didn't notice you were doing it. Now it's time to give yourself permission to put on your favorite clothes, check that mirror, and enjoy the reflection.

Cons are great for a lot of reasons. One of them is they give you a chance to make genuine friends and establish new connections. And of course, this is a major opportunity if you're an emerging writer.

When I attend an event, I want to look (and feel) confident and approachable. I want people to see me and think, "Hey, I'd trust her to read my story and give me feedback," or "Well now, she seems like someone I wouldn't mind sharing a long elevator ride with."

It's also important to me to signal that I'm a "safe" person. A lot of women and other vulnerable individuals travel to conventions alone, and I will always be available to walk them to their rooms, protect their drinks, and hold their bags while they're in the restroom. That, of course, has more to do with demeanor than dress, but no one would ask me for help if they felt too intimidated to come talk to me. (For example, I don't hide my face with a hat or a hood or a Cousin It hairstyle, since that is often read by people as a signal to stay away.)

I go to conventions to participate in what is happening there, to enjoy time with the people I admire and with whom I share a passion for storytelling. I go to be a part of the horror community. And I, like so many in this community, welcome you to do the same.

Now, you.

The next time you're packing for a con, consider these questions:

What are the vibes of this event?

What kind of impression do you want to make?

Whose attention are you trying to attract, and for what purpose? Will your choice of wardrobe, etc. help you do that?

Who do you hope to meet?

What do you want to get out of the experience?

Someone hoping to get a start in a subgenre like splatterpunk might choose different outfits and accessories than someone who wants to publish dark fairy tales. Spending a little time considering whether your look and your goals align is worth doing. Enjoy it.

Pro tips:

-Whatever you choose to wear, make sure it's comfortable. Those spike heels might make you look fabulous, but if they hurt your feet, they aren't worth it. Same goes for dresses you can't bend down in and pants that haven't buttoned comfortably for at least three years.

-Dress in layers, if possible. Cons are held at hotels and event centers, and those rooms are rarely a comfortable temperature, regardless of the season. You might freeze or melt. Bring a jacket or hoodie with you if you're in a t-shirt or tank top; and if you're in a sweater, make sure you have a base layer to peel down to if need be.

-Carry a bag with some cargo room. Dainty purses might be classy, but if you walk by a table of free Advance Review Copies of new releases, you want to be able to snag a few and have a place to put them! Plus people will be handing you bookmarks, postcards, business cards, and more.

-You'll want to have a notebook to write down smart things panelists say and book recommendations. Carry pens for the same reason.

-And, not to sound too much like your mom, but, always have a little snack on you! Sometimes it's hard to find enough time at cons to eat decent meals, and you don't want your first impression to be passing out in front of, like, Ellen Datlow.

Find Your Tribe

Writing can be kinda lonely. When you're typing away, butt in the chair, struggling to get those juicy ideas onto the page (or screen), it's just you and the words.

That makes finding spooky, scribbling friends a vital step toward making this whole horror-writer lifestyle work. You need people who "get" you, who understand the highs and lows you'll encounter on a weekly basis.

In March of 2022, I felt ready to do just that. I had lots of writer friends, but I didn't have horror writer friends, and my dudes, we are a different breed altogether.

So I went straight to the source, and applied to join the Horror Writers Association as an Affiliate Member. I was approved quickly, and joined or followed the HWA social media accounts and channels. I noticed everyone chattering about this huge party called StokerCon, and that year, it was being held in Denver, Colorado. I considered it: could I, an introverted, socially awkward middle-aged woman, fly across the country to stay at a hotel with hundreds of strangers and actually, like, *talk* to them?

My husband, Joel, told me to go for it (I'm super lucky that he supports me in all of this). Then I told myself to go for it. What was I waiting for, anyway, an invitation on thick, creamy paper with cursive lettering? That wasn't coming. So, feeling weird and nervous and probably sweaty, I booked all the tickets: StockerCon, Awards Banquet, plane tickets, and hotel reservation. After that, I freaked out a little, remembering every time I've embarrassed myself in front of strangers (it's a lot of times), but I didn't let myself cancel. Taking the trip was emotionally risky–I barely leave my county–but I was ready to take risks for what I wanted.

Off to Denver I went.

AND. IT. KICKED. ASS.

Yes, it was scary, and overwhelming, and I would have been lost without name tags, but I loved it.

I was a bit starstruck a few times–Lisa Kröger, Brian Keene, Grady Hendrix, and others–but I didn't slip on any banana peels or take any pies to the face.

I made friends! I stayed up late and went to a silly game of Monster Mash and laughed with Shannon Lawrence. I went to the Final Frame Film Festival with Kevin Kennel and Connie Millard, where Kev saw (and heard) me gag. He even cracked up and tapped my arm when the gross part was over (we're still buddies). I went to panel after panel where I got to hear people like Linda Addison and Jamie Flanagan talk about their–I mean *our*–craft.

I bought so many books that it was hard to lug them home. I met Jonathan Gensler, who's still stuck with me for weekly writing sprints.

I went to the StokerCon Awards Banquet and got to see people's dreams come true. (Shoutout to Jerlyn Ford, who buttoned the back of my fancy dress on the elevator because I couldn't reach.)

The last night, Sunday, after most of the revelers had gone home, I visited a horror-themed bar called Slashers with Joseph Wilson and Robert Perez, and after that, we Ubered to a haunted park and howled at the moon (with a bunch of strangers howling back). How's that for a first StokerCon?

The range of horror subgenres represented that weekend was so reassuring; there really is room for everyone! You don't have to "fit in" to fit in. I like to write dark poetry, gothic horror, and ghost stories. So do a lot of other people I met there. And being so at home among Poe fans and splatterpunk writers alike inspired an important realization. The "literary fiction" world had never really wanted me. So why did I ever want to be a part of it? Here was a club of cool kids who welcomed me with open arms (really; I got lots of hugs), and I knew they were my people.

I will add a quick note here to say that not everybody was great. One or two people were kinda middle-school passive-aggressive, in person and online afterward, but meeting them was ultimately helpful, too. It showed me how *not* to treat others.

Leaving StokerCon was like leaving Oz: disorienting and a little sad. I was also overcome by the foggy notion that it may have all been a dream...

It wasn't.

I made friends with other horror writers. And they made friends with me.

Now, you.

I've had a wonderful experience with the Horror Writers Association, and recently moved up to Active Pro Writer membership. (I've also been adopted by the New York chapter, since there is no Buffalo chapter.)

But there are other options, too. A few of these include the Mystery Writers of America (MWA), the Science Fiction & Fantasy Writers Association (SFWA), the Speculative Fiction Writers Association, the Speculative Literature Foundation, and regional and city-specific organizations.

Research these groups to find the best fit for you. Read not only the organizations' websites and social media posts, but also the things people are saying about them. Google the groups, search them on social media, and read reviews. Talk to the members and ask them what they like about belonging.

Then, when you have chosen one and joined up, attend events! Many of these happen online, like meetings, readings, discussion groups, and book clubs. If it's financially feasible, attend their annual gala or festival. If you live near other members, invite them to meet up for coffee. In short, be a joiner. Put yourself out there and remember what your mom told you: be yourself. People will like you.

Bet on Yourself

Making big changes to your lifestyle–even good ones–is scary.

I get it. There is security in repetition. The devil you know is better than the one you don't. Except what if the devil you haven't met yet is so freaking awesome that you'll wonder why you didn't become best friends with them years ago?

And no, we're not satanists; it's just an expression (but send all your complaints to the editor–hee hee.)

My flight home from StokerCon '22 took all day. First I had to wait around in Denver to fly to Atlanta, then sit there for a bit before hopping on a late-night plane ride to Buffalo. I was punch-drunk: deliriously tired, half-asleep on my feet.

But on the jaunt to Buffalo, at about midnight, head nodding in the quiet, dim airplane cabin, a realization struck me like a slap to the face, and I snapped to attention: I had to quit my side job.

Let me step back a minute. I've always had two jobs. Sometimes more. I was born to hustle. My family didn't have a lot of money when I was growing up (six kids, one earning parent), so early on I learned to work for what I wanted and to appreciate what I had. I worked my way through college and then graduate school, keeping my student debt low, earning scholarships when I could, waitressing and bartending (and flag-girling at auctions; nevermind).

The habit, and sometimes the necessity, stuck with me after my MFA graduation in 2011. By then I wasn't behind the bar anymore or slinging trays (to everyone's benefit; I was a really clumsy waitress and have the short-term memory of a goldfish). I got a job as an adjunct professor *and* a part-time job at the local newspaper. Then I quit the newspaper

(I went back later) and got a side job with Leapfrog Press, as the acquisitions editor. That meant I reviewed incoming submissions and either declined them or passed them on to the editor-in-chief. I also helped with other editing and communication tasks as needed, and over several years, I filled different roles at the press–I eventually got too busy to be the acquisitions editor and quit, only to go back as a contest reader and then as an author events coordinator and then, finally, back again as the editor-in-chief when the press was sold to a publisher in the UK. In those years (2012-2022) I also wrote advertorials for a publication called *Buffalo Spree*; wrote lifestyles articles for *Forever Young*, a senior publication; and book reviews for *American Book Review*. For a couple of years I left teaching and worked as a news reporter for the local paper full time, then went back to teaching. I took freelance editing jobs. It was like I made myself work hard enough not to notice what I was missing out on.

But on that plane ride in May 2022, I finally noticed. Not only did I want to be a writer, but I thought I *could* be a writer. I was good enough, and I had the qualities necessary to become better: the hunger for learning, the determination to build my skills, the hesitant but growing confidence in myself. I suddenly realized I could make this work. In short, I had found the faith to bet on myself.

Back home in Western New York, I talked to my husband about leaving my editing job, and he agreed it was the right decision. I gathered my courage for a few days, then broke the news to the publisher. He was disappointed, but understood. Extricating myself took some time, though–we were in the middle of an international manuscript competition–but by August of 2022, I was free, and for the first time in my adult life, I had only one steady, paycheck-earning job.

It was a little terrifying, but also exciting. I had finally gotten out of my own way, and cleared space and time to make my other job–my most *important* job–writing.

Soon enough, when I met new people and they asked me what I did, my answer didn't involve rattling off a string of gigs in order of most-money-making to least-money-making. Not only had my working life changed, but so had my priorities. My answer to "What do you do?" became "I'm a horror writer. And I teach college classes."

I'm a horror writer. I'm a horror writer. I'm a horror writer!

Now, you.

If you decided to bet on yourself, what would that look like?

If you prioritized your writing, what would the risk be?

Is there a safety net, or a measure of emotional security, or a distraction, that you could live without?

For some, the answer is no. They have too many people depending on them to make a move like this. If that is you, it's okay. There is no timeline on this stuff; you can wait until your kids are older or until finances are more stable.

In Chapter 8—Get in the Habit, we'll talk more about making time for writing, with recommendations you can customize for your lifestyle and needs. We all have to do this in our own ways for it to work. The flexibility of these suggestions is the beating heart [beneath the floorboards] of this book.

Believe Beyond the Doubts

Okay. So you've decided you're a writer by this point.

Congratulations!

Now it's time to put some effort into building your confidence and learning to find middle ground between undeserved self-criticism and unhelpful self-aggrandizement.

Building your confidence doesn't happen overnight. Something that helped me was starting therapy during the pandemic lockdown.

I am a recovering people-pleaser. My mom died when I was a kid. We lived in a small town. Everyone was watching us, waiting for us kids to "go bad." So, I learned to be really, really good: good at school, helpful to peers, active in clubs and extracurriculars. It was my way of saying, "See? We're fine!"

Thirty years later, I was an adult who couldn't say no to anyone for anything. All those endless favors, all that donated time, made me resent the people around me (which was not really fair, considering I had trained them how to treat me.) When I stopped being a doormat, I liked myself more. Who'da thunkit? (My therapist. Ha.)

Maybe you don't have the same issues I did (okay, still do, but I'm working on them!); however, I found that liking myself as a person was key to liking myself as a writer and staying confident, even when the rejections rolled in (*more on those in Chapter 13—Embrace the Rejections*).

Confidence doesn't mean arrogance, though. In fact, arrogance will kill your confidence, because it's flimsy, too breakable. There's a lack of honesty to writers who think they know everything about their craft. No one does. To keep evolving, we need to stay humble and keep learning. If you're constantly patting yourself on the back and refusing to recognize growth opportunities, you're missing out on chances to improve your writing skills (plus, no one will want to trade feedback with you, and that's no fun).

Just as toxic, though, is an inner critic who tells you you'll never get it right. That's the voice that says you should quit before you've even tried. Tell that voice to zip it.

Easier said than done, I know.

One way to cope with that negative voice is to cut a deal: "Okay, let me finish this story/poem/novel and then you can rip it apart for ten minutes straight." Another way is to say, "Okay, go ahead and tell me everything that is wrong with my writing for five minutes, but I have the bullshit detector on and if you can't make a solid case, you shush and let me work." You'll see how often that voice actually has nothing to offer.

If, however, the voice does point out that in Chapter Two, the hero lost the rope she's going to need to defeat the monster in Chapter Eight, thank the voice, go back to Chapter Two and put that damn rope in her backpack. Then take yourself and that voice to the kitchen for cookies. Or wine. Whatever–get a treat.

You can also make great strides in building confidence by avoiding negative comparisons. It's so easy to see people announcing publication after publication on social media, or to read the work of amazing writers in magazines and journals and anthologies, and think, "That'll never be me."

For one thing, each of those successful people had to get their start, too. They weren't born getting these publications. They wrote draft after draft, did revision after revision, just like you're doing now. Do your best not to be jealous of those folks, not to envy their success, but to be genuinely happy for them. Because if they could do it, you can do it, too. What can you learn from them? What can their writing show you? Do they teach any classes or workshops you can take? Are they doing a public reading you can attend? Do they have interviews or podcast appearance recordings available online? You can benefit from all of this.

For another thing, they aren't you. Corny as it may sound, everyone has their own path to take, with their own roadblocks, detours, and shortcuts. Privilege is real. Some of us have access to formal education while others have to self-teach. Some can travel to conventions; others don't have the available funds or are full-time caretakers. If aspiring authors have an "in," well that's a leg up on those of us who don't. (Consider this example–Joe Hill is the son of famous authors Tabitha and Stephen King. Dude's a great author, but don't tell me his mom and pop didn't give him a boost! Yes, he did change his name to Joe Hill, credit for that, but word eventually got out and how could it not have helped? On the other hand, what if word got out and he wasn't as good as he is? The negative comparisons would have been shattering. While connections might open doors, only good work will keep them open.)

Stick to your own path and don't worry about being "outpaced" by anyone else. It's not a race.

Now, you.

Unpack your baggage to find out just what you're carrying around with you and why it's so heavy.

If you don't have access to therapy, that's okay. Open up your journal and think on the page. What's putting the hitch in your giddy-up? What makes you doubt yourself? Write it down. Make a list. And then spend some time thinking about each item. Where do those negative feelings come from? Are they based on evidence, or is your anxiety *lying* to you? If there's a habit you've developed that isn't serving you, what steps can you take to self-correct?

Sometimes it's a defense mechanism that we should outgrow. After my mom died, I started withdrawing and dissociating during social situations as part of my "pretend to be fine" act. I brought the habit into my adulthood, and instead of protecting me, it just made me seem antisocial and unapproachable. Now, I work on being more outgoing.

Then, as a related activity, ask yourself how your overall confidence or lack thereof affects your confidence as a writer. Are you afraid people will laugh at your ideas? Don't be–in the world of horror and speculative fiction, the more bizarre, the better. Imagine Stephen King pitching some of his ideas to Tabitha across the breakfast table. It might have sounded like this:

SK: "So in this next one, there's an evil entity, okay?"

TK: "I'm with you."

SK: "And at first it's a clown."

TK: "Ooh! Scary. I hate clowns."

SK: "Me too. And he lives in the sewer."

TK: "The sewer..."

SK: "Yeah. The clown lives in the sewer. And he, like, eats kids or something. I'll work it out."

TK: "He eats..."

SK: "Kids. Yeah. And they fight him and then, like, other stuff happens, and *then* he turns into a spider!"

TK: "He was a clown but now he's a spider?"

SK: "Uh huh."

TK: "Sounds like another best seller!"

SK: "Hell, yeah."

(Then they clink their coffee cups together.)

If it's your writing skills themselves you're worried about, well hell, that's fixable. Go back to Chapter Two and read it again.

If it's helpful, come up with a mantra and whisper it to yourself over and over, out loud or in your head. You can make it corny: *Write every day and you improve in every way*. OR you can make it more personal: *I don't have to write the best, just my best*. Whatever works for you. (I have one, but I won't tell you what it is. I will say that it makes me feel like something both ancient and eternal, with teeth the size of tree branches.)

You'll come up with one that works for you–a phrase that reminds you of your own power and capability.

(If it takes you a while to settle on one, just play the song "I'm Still Standing" by Elton John over and over in the meantime. That works, too.)

Get in the Habit

Making writing a regular habit (and not a task on a to-do list) will keep you writing.

Don't let this become another well-intended resolution, like those "I'll exercise five times a week" New Year's "promises" that you break by the second week of January.

To work writing time into your schedule, be practical and realistic, and ignore the bullshit advice out there that says you must write something like 5,000 words a day or don't you dare call yourself a wordsmith.

Even after I quit my editing job, I struggled to find time to write. I still do–I probably always will. No week will ever be the same for me. I'm a busy gal, and my "doings" change with the seasons–semester ramp-ups in late summer and mid-winter, intermittent grading marathons; late-spring garden installation and early fall canning the fruits (and vegetables) of my labor.

During those periods, I might not find time to do much more than check my submissions lists and make a few notes for my novel.

In a good week, though–during the darkest days of winter, the longest days of summer, or a grading drought mid semester–I'll spend five hours writing and revising.

In a great week, I'll spend twenty.

And it's not just about finding the time, is it? It's about finding the *energy* to write, and sometimes, that's the more elusive of the two.

At the end of most days, I'm fried. I've spent too much time performing my role of energetic teacher, of friendly colleague, to have anything left when I get home. I just want to hug my cat until he gets sick of it and attacks me, make a crappy dinner, and veg out on the couch.

I have more energy in the mornings, before teaching classes, so I fit an hour or so of writing in on the days that I can. I have time on the weekends. Rarely, I am in the mood to write in the evenings, and I might even cheat my bedtime a little if I'm on a roll.

Some of my friends have stricter minimums: they make themselves write 1,000 words a day, or 500, even if they delete them all the next day. And kudos to them! But I'm too much of a scatterbrain to set those goals for myself. If I did, I'd just end up feeling bad about myself when I couldn't reach them.

I write the same way I consume cheese: as much as I can, as often as I can.

Now, you.

I have found the best way to find pockets of time and energy is to make a week-long schedule on paper, with columns for each day.

First, block out your typical obligations, like work and picking up children and making dinner and running errands. Oh–and sleep. Can't forget sleep! What's left, in theory, should be your free time.

Then, track your energy levels for a week, making notes in those windows of free time with your highs and lows. Pick out the patterns. If, like me, you can't muster the ol' razzle-dazzle after 5 p.m. on weekdays, be honest and mark that down. But if you get a second wind from, like, 8 to 10 p.m., hey! Maybe that could be your writing time.

Identify your time wasters. How many minutes (or hours) a day do you spend doom-scrolling through social media posts from people you barely know? How many reruns of *Rick & Morty* do you binge per night before deciding you need some sleep? How many times do you put luxury items, like $49 scratch-off horror movie posters, in your Amazon cart, only to take them back out again because, what the hell, who can spend $49 on a poster that doesn't even come *framed*?

I bet you can't answer "zero" to all three of the above questions. So can you take even a fraction of that wasted time and repurpose it into this wonderful, bad-ass thing you want to do? Into this wonderful, bad-ass writer you want to be?

I hope you're nodding your head right now.

Something else to consider is getting your family or roommates on board. If you say you're going to write between 8 and 10 p.m., but your partner knocks on the door every five minutes asking what you did with the remote control or what the dish full of green, moldy sludge in the back of the fridge used to be, well, you won't get much done.

Be upfront and honest. Tell them you need to take this time–whatever time you are able to set aside–to spend with the characters in your head. Hang a Do Not Disturb sign up. Put on headphones.

And if none of that works, rethink your writing location. One of my friends writes in her attic. Another goes to the library. I see cool people writing in coffee shops, tapping away while they take breaks to sip their chai-somethings.

Writers write. That's it. So if you want to be a writer, you have to find the time and energy and space to put your butt in a chair and get words on the page.

Trust the Process

As I tell my students all the time, writing is a process, with steps that are less like steps and more like a game of Chutes & Ladders, because it's just as likely that we'll slide backward as move forward.

First, there's reading–seeking inspiration and examples of what you want to try (and honestly, confirmation of styles that don't fit your writing voice–that's important, too).

There's prewriting–that's freewriting, outlining, making character sketches and timelines, researching any topics that require more than general knowledge. When you are satisfied with an *idea*, you move on to drafting, which is shaping that idea into a story, with cause and effect, character details, setting description, action and dialogue, etc.

After that, there's usually some re-drafting, going back through what you have and smoothing out the rough edges. Do this until you have a version you are willing to share with a trusted writing friend or small group. (Sometimes your first readers, who give you feedback on your draft, are called "beta readers.") You can call that step sharing or workshopping or getting feedback. Once you have that feedback, spend some time thinking about it, being open to the ideas, and considering which suggestions you want to try out.

Next comes the hardest part and the part that is most fun: Revising! Improve your story. Make the reality of what's on the page more closely match the successful vision that lives in your head.

Now revise it 700 more times. For real. Revise it a lot, giving yourself time in between working on it. Share it again if you want to. Read it out loud to yourself or to your cat if they're willing to listen. Look for contradictions and plot holes and inconsistencies. Look for parts that are boring or confusing–the two cardinal sins of fiction writing.

When you think it's amazing, move on. The next step is line editing. That means looking at every sentence, asking yourself if you want to change any diction or syntax or punctuation.

(A couple of tips for line editing: get rid of adverbs where you can, and choose a better verb. "Walked hesitatingly" is clunky and weird. "Tip-toed" or "edged" or "crept" is way better–cleaner and clearer. Also, readers get lost in super-long sentences. Break those up.)

Once you love all of your sentences, proofread for errors and typos. Check formatting, spacing, capitalization, etc. Messy manuscripts often get rejected by publishers right away–though that may seem unfair, consider this: many small publishers and micro presses don't have the resources to edit submitters' work on a granular level. Also, sloppy copy may signal–inaccurately–that you don't care much about what you're putting out in the world. So, don't skip this step! Give yourself a cookie for every mistake you find.

Does that seem like a lot to go through? IT IS.

Which is why you better love every minute of it. Because writing is the whole process, not just those magical moments when you get a new idea or come up with the perfect analogy to describe a hangover. If you don't love the hard parts of writing, you won't love writing, and you'll end up discouraged.

I have learned to find joy in the whole dang shebang. That wasn't instant for me–as a young writer, even in my grad school years, getting feedback was tough: *What do you mean my first draft isn't perfect and worthy of awards?!* Okay, I wasn't quite that delusional, but, it took time to appreciate feedback from my mentors and peers. I had a negative impression of "criticism." (I don't like that word–it *is* negative–so I don't use it in my own writing classes. "Feedback" is more friendly and more accurate.)

But now, I see feedback as full of potential for improving the story! Feedback is a list of ideas to try and possible solutions for the weak spots in my stories. Feedback is a compliment–someone thinks my work is worth their reading time and creative problem-solving effort. Feedback is a gift, and should be accepted in that spirit.

And revision? Revision is powerful and makes me feel like a badass. When I revise, my story transforms before my eyes. Like, am I a wizard? Did I conjure this? Yes and yes. And then I sit back and read it and get to be proud of myself–I made this thing! It started as a blank page and now it's this living, breathing story!

What's not to like?

Now, you.

I'm afraid experience is the best teacher when it comes to the writing process. You have to get used to it in order to appreciate it.

But there are ways to avoid writing process self-destruction.

Do not set unrealistic deadlines. Each step is going to take as long as it takes. When my siblings and I whined about long car rides or lateness as kids, my dad would say, "We'll get there when we get there." The same logic applies here–if you rush a step, or (*gasp!*) skip one, you're only cheating yourself and the quality of your work.

Rethink your ideas about progress. Taking a step back because you need to improve an aspect of your story before moving forward is progress. Deleting an entire scene or chapter because it doesn't serve your vision is progress. Hell–deciding you don't like the story you've already spent 20 hours on and abandoning it is progress, too, because you can move on to other ideas. (Abandoning every story or even *most* stories–well, that's not progress, that's dodging the challenging but rewarding revision and polish part of any story's evolution; but some tales do fall on the march to publishing. I put those ones in what I call "cold storage." They aren't exactly dead, but they're not alive and kicking.)

Reward yourself along the way, not just when you have a complete, polished, impressive final draft. Pat yourself on the back. Give yourself a gold star. Whatever tangible little treat makes you feel happy. (My favorites are cheese and chocolate, though *usually* not together.)

Here is a promise I will make you: If you learn to love the writing process, you will become a better writer.

And isn't that why you bought this book?

Do the Research, Part 1: Stories

I admit with no shame that I'm a research nerd. I love it.

Somewhere along my meandering educational path, a writing teacher of mine (Who? Can't remember. Sorry!) taught me about the importance of "proofs," little details that make your stories more authentic and give you credibility as a writer. For example, if you're writing about changing a tire, write about the jack and the lug wrench, how some lug nuts come off easily and others are rusted on. Because "he loosened up the screw thingies with the bar thing that's shaped like a cross after lifting the car up with the thing that lifts cars up" makes it seem like you've never even seen a tire before.

It's fine to take that old piece of advice to "write what you know." I've done it–written stories that feature bartender and waitress protagonists, stories set on golf courses and in gardens. But I wanted more. More subject matter. More diversity of character. More options when it came to setting and plot. Because there were limits, of course, to what I already knew, I saw that if I only ever wrote what I knew, my stories would soon be boring as butterless toast.

So I "revised" that piece of advice. The updated version goes like this:

Write what you know, and if you don't know,
do some research so that–BOOM–you do know.

There's not a form of research I don't like. I'll get books from the library (extra points for me if I have to acquire them through Interlibrary Loan). I can spend all day chasing information online, falling down more than one Google rabbithole. I'll visit places to get a sense of their layout and topography. But my FAVORITE, favorite *favorite* way to research is to talk to people who know more about the subject I'm researching than me.

I know this method won't be for everyone. Some folks are painfully shy or introverted; they'd rather do a shot of ghost pepper hot sauce than speak to a stranger. Young adults, who do much of their social interaction online (and who were stuck in their bedrooms for two years during Covid lockdown), might not feel comfortable asking questions about someone else's life or job or hobby.

But lemme tell you. There is no better way to pick up important, realistic details for your characters, settings, and plots than talking to people who work those jobs and interact with those places and live those experiences. Talking to an expert in a specific career or field can provide you with jargon (job lingo), inside jokes, knowledge of processes, and show you things like body language and attitude. All aspects of a conversation can help your story.

Plus it's fun.

(I was a reporter, remember? Curiosity was quite literally part of my job, and I took it as a personal challenge to get reticent public officials–who wouldn't talk to other reporters–to sing like canaries for me. When you are exploring the details of your stories and characters, you are doing essentially what a reporter does. And you know what? Most people love talking about themselves and their jobs, so this part will prove easier than you might think.)

There's one story I wrote, "Damp in the Walls," (one of my favorites), that required tons of information I didn't have. I needed to know about pregnancy, and the kinds of doctor appointments a pregnant person would go to, and what would happen at those appointments and who would be there in the exam room. I needed to know about architecture–what kinds of houses were built on fieldstone basements, and in what era, and what their general styles and layouts would be. (If you're curious, and you're probably not, fieldstone basements were popular until about 1915–two stories, wooden frame.) I also had to learn about weather, and how rain affects certain kinds of topographies; I needed to learn about floods. I had to understand how to portray patterns of domestic abusers accurately. Oh! And I had to learn how fast a person with a compound leg fracture could drown alone in cold, dark, rising water.

To begin my info-gathering process, I hit my network of close friends and family.

My oldest buddy Lindsey (who I pestered into being my best friend in sixth grade), was pregnant at the time with her youngest. She answered all my preggo questions. For fieldstone basement stuff, I hit up Lawrence M. Schwab, Sr. (That's my dad. He worked in construction as a young man and his brothers were builders.) Kelly Sundberg, my friend from grad school, wrote about her experiences with domestic abuse in the book *Goodbye, Sweet Girl,* and is open about her experiences during public speaking engagements and in essays–she was a sensitivity reader for those sections, making sure I got them (horrifically) true to life. For the how-long-would-it-take-to-die material, I went to my friend Julie, who works as a physician's assistant in an emergency room (and who used to work at a surgeon's office, fixing people with sports-type bone injuries). She's super smart and answers lots of my blood-and-guts questions, as does Leah, a friend who is a registered nurse (and horror fan!).

Then I came to the weather and flooding questions. And no one in my inner circle had that knowledge. But I remembered that in 2009, there was severe flooding in my county that washed away homes and even killed a couple people. It was called a "hundred-year flood," and took everyone by surprise.

I needed someone who knew about *that* flood. Someone on the inside–a government or municipal worker who saw the devastation first hand and had to actually deal with it.

So I went to Facebook, asking something like: "Does anyone know anyone who knows a lot about storms and flooding? Like what happened here in 2009?"

I didn't have to wait long. A lovely person I know through dog rescue, Kelly (different Kelly), popped up and said something like: "My husband Jake works for the county and had to deal with all that!" And I asked her if he would talk to me. He said yes, so we arranged a phone call.

I think I kept him on for about an hour, asking stuff like "How much rain has to fall per square inch, and how fast does it have to fall, to create a flood?" and "Could a flood like the one in 2009 uproot trees and smash them into houses?" and "What would the damage look like afterward?" etc. etc. etc. Like I said, I'm a curious little cat.

Meow.

And I got everything I needed for my story.

I acknowledge my good luck here. I know a lot of people who know a lot of things–I've got smarty-pantses to the left and right of me. My sister's a lawyer. My brother's an engineer. My friend works for Child Protective Services. Her husband is in law enforcement. My brother-in-law's close friend is a geologist, who answered a bunch of questions about a specific region (and its mineral deposits) in the state of Georgia.

No one has refused to talk to me yet. I'm not saying it won't happen, but in general, people like talking about what they do and what they know. They're happy to help. They like the idea of their information contributing to a piece of art–even, in the case of "Damp in the Walls," a weird story about sentient ghostly floodwaters that may or may not be capable of residential allyship.

The cool thing is, once you start thinking about your family, circle of friends, neighbors, work associates, and so on, you will see how many people you know who know things you might not know as much about. And almost all of them secretly want to talk about what they know.

Now, you.

Do your best to reframe your ideas about research.

It's not homework. No one is asking you to use parenthetical citations. There's no grade on this. Instead, it's a treasure hunt! It's a quest. A real-life video game whereby you collect not rings nor gold coins but little bits of knowledge and accuracy that will take your stories from good to great.

Do a mental run-down of your friends and family. What are they experts in? What do they know that you don't? Could you put any of *their* talents and interests to work for *your* stories?

Another approach: What patterns do you already see in your fiction? Do you write about the same type of protagonist again and again? The same setting? *Who* else, and *what* else, and *where* else do you want to write about? Establish that, then go find someone willing to tell you about it. It's easier than you think.

If you're shy, here's a little script you can fill in with your particulars:

You: *"Hello, my name is [awesome author] and I hear that you have a lot of experience with [unknown thing/place]. I'm writing a story about [unknown thing/place], and I wondered if you could spare a few moments to talk with me? We could chat on the phone or I could buy you a cup of coffee down at [local diner]."*

Them: *"Thanks, I would love to!"*

You: *"Great! Thank you!"*

And if that doesn't work, you can always surf the interwebs or visit your local library.

Do the Research, Part 2: Submissions Opportunities

Once you have polished drafts that you're proud of, it's time to find homes for those strange tales.

This involves research that's a different kind of fun and (bonus!) record keeping. Also, parameters.

Research first. (Should I get a tattoo that says that?) There are some great websites and e-newsletters that post submissions opportunities. For horror and speculative open calls, I like The Horror Tree (horrortree.com) and Angelique Fawns's blog (www.fawns.ca). A more general, but larger list of monthly submissions opportunities can be found at Erica Verillo's blog, publishedtodeath.blogspot.com. Brian Keene offers Jobs in Hell (paid subscription) on Substack, where you can also find Angela Yuriko Smith's Authortunities (part free/part paid subscription).

I tend to check these lists when they come out at the beginning of each month. If I see calls I want to submit stories to, I mark down the days they open or close in my calendar, so I don't miss an important date. (If a publication is open for a limited window, try to submit early–if they are only going to take one bloody revenge story, you want it to be *your* bloody revenge story.) FYI, my calendar is a colorful, stapled-spine, cheap paper planner I got at the dollar store. Something about it being in print, in my hands, helps me remember to look at it. I carry it to work and back every day. Some people keep their calendars on their phones, and that's great, too. Find what works for you.

Always check submissions details on the publishers' websites, though. I have submitted work to a magazine before based on someone's submissions list only to get back a message that–*womp womp*–the publisher isn't actually open. Oops!

Aside from reading submissions lists, I also search for open calls on social media, checking the accounts of magazines, journals, podcasts, and presses that I admire. (You can also go right to their websites. Usually there is a "Submissions" tab or button to click on for details.) On Facebook, I'm a member of groups and pages that announce sub calls. (A good one is "OPEN CALL: Speculative Markets - Horror, Science Fiction, and Fantasy.")

I do my best to only send out polished, absolutely done stories and poems for publication consideration. But, I'm a "fiddler," so I have been known to submit a story on a Wednesday and then line edit it, again, on a Thursday. From the first rejection to the ultimate acceptance, any one of my stories has likely morphed, in small ways, a few times. I tell myself it's not indecision–it's evolution!

Anywho. All those submissions I send out? I gotta keep track of them.

I do this in three ways.

I have a (free) Submittable account (submittable.com), and any magazines, presses, and journals that require Submittable submissions (because *they* pay for accounts) are tracked there. Nice, because when a press clicks open my submission, my little button goes from "received" to "in progress." Sadly, that doesn't necessarily mean someone's actually reading it. But it's fun to check my account several times a day, hoping those buttons will change. "Staring at Submittable" is one of my hobbies.

Then there is The Grinder (thegrinder.diabolicalplots.com), which is a donation-run site. The Grinder is not like Submittable–it's not a site through which writers send their work to publishers. It's just for writers' record keeping. So, I add my submissions in, with details like the dates of each submission and titles of stories, and when I get responses (rejections or acceptances), I go back and update those records. (It's exciting when I can click "personal rejection" instead of "form rejection," and of course, even better when I can click "Accepted!") The Grinder doesn't have all markets on file, though–if a magazine, podcast, journal, press, etc. is new, it might not yet appear on The Grinder's list of options (though you can suggest markets for the site to add). The Grinder is awesome because it posts information like the number of days it typically takes a publisher to answer, what percentage of submissions are accepted, and how many pending submissions the press has yet to decide upon. Of course, all of this is only based on data entered by users of The Grinder. (The Grinder can also help you *find* markets, which is very cool.)

So, because Submittable and The Grinder are limited (The Grinder less so than Submittable), I have to keep a third log of submissions. Most logical adult people alive in this century would do this on a computer, in an Excel spreadsheet or something that's super easy to update. There'd be columns and rows and different fonts and colors. It would be an organizational marvel.

But me?

I like to be old-fashioned sometimes. I keep a messy, weird, handwritten log in a paper notebook, unhelpfully mixed in with story notes and workshop feedback, marked by Post-it notes. I have six columns: Submission fee (if there is one), Title (of my work), Genre, Publication/Anthology/Press, and Response. Are the columns straight? No. Can I sometimes not read my handwriting? Yes.

But it gets better (and by that I mean worse). When I get an acceptance, I will write that down and then highlight the word with an actual yellow marker. If I get a personalized rejection, I put a little star next to the word "Rejected" and then I circle the star and I color in the circle with a purple marker. Updating this log, which now spans THREE separate notebooks (going back to 2021), takes forever and involves a lot of page flipping. So I came up with a modification: If every submission on a page has gotten a response, I put a big X in the bottom right corner! See? Not-easy-peasy-but-I-do-it-to-please-me. (What can I say? It's fun to color things in.)

If I submit a story or poem to more than one place, and it gets accepted by a publisher, I go to my various submissions logs and find out where I need to send polite withdrawal emails.

Now, you.

Open a free account on Submittable and donate a few bucks to The Grinder so you can jump on there, too. Additionally, start your own submissions log in whatever way you want to–the organized, searchable computer way or the higgledy-piggledy pen-and-paper way.

Pick a few days a month or an hour or two a week to research submissions opportunities. Put parameters around your search time, because it can be kind of addicting. Mark important dates on your calendar. Be careful about which publishers allow simultaneous submissions (and it's totally understandable if you'd rather not submit to those places–I don't, unless they promise short turn-around times).

Have a short, current biographical statement ready to go. Some places say keep it to 100 words, some only want 50. If you're just starting out, it's fine to have something like "Ronald Coolkid writes horror and fantasy. He lives in Upstate Lower Mid Pennsylvania with his cat, Bobsled." As you get publications to your name, you can add them to your bio, eventually including only the most recent or the ones you're most proud of. (Don't worry. The ones that get bumped will still be on your website!)

Keep your submissions emails short and sweet. Look up the name of the editor, when possible, and address the email to them. Here's an example:

Dear Christopher,

Thank you for considering my story, "The Quilting Circle of Bygone Gardens," for *Soul Scream Antholozine*. It is about 6,400 words long. I hope you enjoy it.

Sincerely,

Rebecca Cuthbert

(Follow each publisher's guidelines for subject lines. If they have no preference, just include the word "Submission," along with your story title and name.)

My friend West commented that sending out submissions is like "sending little missives of hope" out into the world.

You'll find out soon that she's right.

Make Friends Online

It's no surprise to anyone reading this that the word "horror" often frightens folks away (especially the top-to-toe normies). Most of us have had the following exchange when meeting new people:

You: "Hello, I'm [name]."

Them: "Hi! Great to meet you! What do you do?"

You: "I write horror."

Them: "Oh..."

The conversation stalls there. They're not sure what to say or how to react, and most of them probably have no idea that horror contains more cross-genres and subgenres than we can count. They hear "horror" and think "Bad. Scary. Must run away." Sadly, they don't stay long enough to hear our hot takes on (fictional) cannibalism (ha!).

Point is: it can be hard to make new friends...*unless* you go online!

The spooky folks–the Halloween People–are probably the friendliest bunch to ever congregate on social media.

(I should stop here and tell you I'm not a social media guru. I don't have thousands of followers or weekly viral posts. But what I *do* have are genuine friends and authentic interactions with folks I've met online through our shared interest in creepy literature.)

I first found them on what was Twitter, and is now X. Obviously that platform has gone through a lot of change, but when I first joined up, I followed writers and publishers I knew of and admired, then liked and commented on their posts. I told them congratulations and I shared their good news about publications, awards, and events. I adhered to the classic advice on how to make friends anywhere, in any community: "To make a friend, you have to be a friend."

Soon, the people I talked to talked back. I noticed other cool people in the comments sections, and followed them. Someone posted about a Zoom happy hour, and I sort of invited myself. That happy hour became a workshop, where I got to meet other awesome people. Then I got invited to a couple of groups on the social media platform Discord, wherein I made more friends, eventually trading work for peer feedback. (To do that, I had to get brave and raise my emoji hand on a message thread of folks who were looking to trade writing critiques.) After I had been on that platform for some time, an editor putting together an independently published anthology put out an invitation for story proposals. I'm happy to say he thought my story cut the mustard!

I also joined some closed groups on Facebook, which, like Discord groups, are a bit "cozier" and offer more of an opportunity to get to know the other members. Some of those were suggested to me by Facebook's algorithms, and I asked their moderators to join them. Others I was invited to by writer friends who thought I'd enjoy the company.

And holy wow. Has that support network been vital.

Like, if I post something close to "How many corpses is too many corpses for one medium-sized ghoul to eat?" in/on one of my horror writers' groups, chats, or pages, I'm going to get numbers and follow-up questions: "Are the corpses fresh or old? Two if fresh, three if old. How long has it been since the ghoul's last meal? Are there condiments or side dishes?" Etc. If I just wrote that same question on my regular feeds, with no audience filters, I'm going to freak out my family and my coworkers won't say hello in the hallway anymore. Let's not even discuss calls from the FBI.

My online friends–who are *real* friends–are there for me in ways that some of my non-horror-writer-friends can't be. Not because those other friends aren't awesome and kind, but because they don't know what it's like to make it a whole TWELVE hours with a submission at *The Dark* before getting a rejection (throw the biodegradable confetti), or how much it stings to get a final-round "thanks but no thanks" from a dream pub on the story you wrote just for them (pass the tissues).

There are so many benefits to finding safe online spaces to interact with folks from your community and make new friends. You can encourage one another, commiserate on bad days, celebrate good news together, share submissions calls, trade feedback, start Zoom workshops, host writing sprints, and more.

My online writer buddies just *get* me.

And I get them back.

Now, you.

Go to your favorite social media platform. Using the search bar, put in some keyword-type hashtags, like #horror, #horrorwriting, #darkfiction, #horrorbooks, #horrorfam, #gothic, #ghoststory, etc. You can search for your favorite genres and subgenres, authors you love, and horror or speculative writers' groups you want to check out.

Once you've found several accounts to follow, interact with them! Comments do not need to be professions of undying loyalty or novella-length motivational speeches. If, like, Quill & Crow Publishing House posts that they have a new book available for preorder, and it looks cool, write "This looks cool!" or "Will put this on my TBR list!" Often, the person posting will thank you, or like your comment, and eventually, those you follow will follow you back, and then you'll meet others through them, and you'll like and comment on *their* stuff, and you'll meet others through them, and...

You see the pattern.

Amongst all this new social media activity, keep your eyes out for joining opportunities and do the online version of raising your hand. If someone says, "Hey, thinking about starting a little horror writers' happy hour. Maybe once a month? Who's in?" then you type "ME!" or "I'd love to join!" If someone posts "Splatter authors, join my Facebook group!" say "Okay!" and then click "Join." Soon enough, you'll have such valuable relationships with horror buddies cast far and wide that you'll wonder how you ever lived without them.

Embrace the Rejections

Getting work rejected is tough.

I get it.

I've been there. And I am there. And I'll always be there.

Because getting work rejected is part of being a writer! (At least until a writer is super famous. Like, no one is rejecting Grady Hendrix. He's *Grady Hendrix*. Editors would arm-wrestle to get his work into their anthologies.)

Like most writers getting their start, I used to submit stories to a few places–literally a *few*. And of course they got rejected, because that's the most likely outcome of submitting stories to any market. (Take a moment to absorb that hard truth, because it's a fact of life for all but probably 0.00001 percent of writers. Accepting rejection as part of doing business in this industry will save you *so* much pain, as I eventually learned.)

At the time, though, I felt *bad* when I got those no-thank-yous–like my work wasn't good enough, or my style wasn't trendy enough, or I myself was too much of a nobody for any editor to want my stories.

That changed when I saw the "#100rejections" hashtag on social media. I was curious; I did some Googling. And what I found was an excellent article from *Literary Hub* by writer Kim Laio. You can find it here: What Collecting 100 Rejections Taught Me About Creative Failure < Literary Hub (lithub.com). The gist of the article is this: aim to get 100 rejections a year. Celebrate your growing number as the months go by; make a game of it; collect them like gold stars. Because if you get a hundred rejections in a year, odds are that you'll get some acceptances, too.

Because guess what?

Rejections are very rarely a commentary on the quality of your writing.

Stories get rejected for all of the following reasons and more:

-The story didn't fit the publication's/issue's theme or ideal.

-The editors had already accepted a story similar in plot or tone or setting.

-The slush reader who opened your submission didn't fall in love with the story.

-The story was super good but the slush readers or editors just liked others more.

-The story, while within guidelines, was too long or too short for the remaining space in that particular issue.

-Editors got so many submissions that only one or three or five percent of stories submitted made it in.

-Etc.

There is no magic formula for getting stories accepted. Sure, you should send out only your best work, follow guidelines, and make sure each story is a good fit for the publication you send it to, but, beyond that, you don't have any control over the situation. It's all subjective, and acceptances are based on circumstances and variables that much of the time, you can't even guess at.

So, like a fisherman/woman/person who can't predict which way a school of fish will swim, cast a wide net. That's what #100rejections is all about–giving your work as many chances as possible to be noticed and accepted, and recognizing that even rejections mean progress toward finding your work a home.

Since adopting this practice for myself mid-year in 2021, I've really racked 'em up. That year, I sent out 55 submissions total, with six of those being accepted. I did the (simple) math, which came out to something like 10 percent of submissions being accepted. Applying that projection, in 2022, I sent out 160 submissions. Know how many were accepted? Sixteen! I kid you not. And one of them was for a whole book! (*In Memory of Exoskeletons,* Alien Buddha Press, March 2023). I'm a confirmed 10-percent-acceptance-rate gal, and proud of it.

As I write this, it's November of 2023, and I've sent out 99 submissions so far for the year. I'm sure I'll get in another dozen or so, and while I won't reach my 2022 record, I'll still be pretty happy: I've gotten 11 acceptances and about 70 rejections (with more on the way). My percentage is holding.

With this volume of submissions, individual rejections don't usually sting (and if I get a personalized rejection from an editor, that's a little treat!). There's still the occasional disappointment–the rejected story I wrote *just* for that sub call, or the form R (boilerplate rejection) from a press I thought would be a perfect home for my novella manuscript–but those disappointments don't lead to discouragement.

And, as for the very rare case in which I *am* actually sad, I have a rule, which also came from my friend West: I can be bummed out for a day. Then it's time to cheer up and go back to the business of gettin' after it.

There was one such instance not long ago. I had sent a collection of stories to a tiny UK press that seemed to publish speculative fiction. It was early days for the press; the editors had only published their own titles up to that point, but I didn't see that as an issue–all presses start somewhere, and self-publishing is absolutely a route a lot of successful authors take. I also thought of how neat it would be to get in on the ground floor of a new publishing house.

Well, the rejection eventually came in from those editors, and it came in with, um...flair? Is that what I want to call it? No. It came in with some real rudeness: a rejection/insult combo that left me feeling like utter garbage. I won't recount the entire message here, but it included the statement that my writing was "a dime a dozen" and that I was nothing special.

Let no one call me dishonest. My dudes, it made me cry.

The evening I got the email, my niece and nephew were over at our house for a game night. Because I didn't want them to see me upset (they are empathetic little sweeties), Aunt Becky took a time-out and snuck off to her bedroom to do a little private boo-hooing.

Later that night, I shared the rejection email in one of those closed online groups I talked about in the last chapter. My friends there validated my feelings, agreed that the rejection was needlessly mean, and assured me it was inaccurate, as well. Their support, alongside my own down-but-not-out sense of creative self-worth, helped me put that rejection behind me and since then, it's become a source of strength. As actor Michael Cain said, I "use[d] the difficulty." It made me tougher. The next time I get a rejection that tells me, explicitly or implicitly, that I'm a no-talent hack, I'll take a moment to pity the editor, record the response, and save my tears for a worthier cause.

Now, you.

Part of improving your attitude toward rejections is desensitization: getting more rejections. And to get more rejections you have to send out more submissions.

If you are still pretty new to this, you don't have to set a #100rejections goal right away. Build up to it. Start at 25 rejections (which means more than 25 submissions.) You can do that! (Go back to Chapter 11-Do the Research, Part 2: Submissions for tips on finding submissions opportunities.) Chances are, you'll sail past that goal. Then, the next year, up your goal to 50 rejections. Keep going. You'll find, like I did, that you get to celebrate acceptances along the way. Before you know it, you'll get a rejection, and think "Ooh! One step closer to my next acceptance!" (Remember being a kid and saving up bar codes or box tops until you had enough to send out for the little toy advertised on the back of a cereal box? Yeah. It's like that!)

And all of this is so much more easily done if you've already followed the steps recommended in earlier chapters–if you can see your skills improving through educational pursuits, if you invest time in the whole writing process, if you have a community to support you (and gamify rejections with you), if you recognize that each submission opportunity is just one fun-size Crunch bar in a whole trick-or-treat bag's worth of publication possibilities.

Now set yourself a goal and go get those Rs!

Dump the Negative Nellies

I've been disappointed to find that, in and among a 99-percent-cool community, there are a few people who love nothing more than stealing others' joy and making them feel bad one way or another.

I am not talking about friends who need to vent about hardships or bad news or a particularly rough rejection. I'm not talking about brave people who whistleblow about abuse or harassment or mistreatment.

I'm talking about the folks who throw pity parties for themselves on the reg and either want you to spend all your time reassuring them or want you to put your name alongside theirs on the party invitation.

I am not interested in doing either. Because that crap is contagious and leads to self-defeat.

I promise this is related:

Once, I started a book club with a couple friends. I thought it would be awesome. And for three or four months, it was. We had snacks and talked about books and nerded out. But then. *Then*. Members invited friends who invited friends, and soon "book club" became "complain about your kids' stepparents and teachers club."

I quit.

And when I got more serious about my writing, I joined public writers' groups on Facebook with hundreds of members–places with names like "Writers Who Want to Support Other Writers" and "Writers United for Success" and "Fiction Writers Central" (those aren't their exact names, wink)–with that same book-club-starting enthusiasm.

And I left most of those groups, because instead of support forums and resource-sharing spaces, they became pages filled with posts like "I don't know why no one will publish me it's so unfair," and "Why am I bothering with this I got three rejections on my story writing is just a waste of time," or my least favorite: "My novel died on sub."

Oof.

If folks want to quit when they've barely even started, they absolutely can. That is their right. Maybe they will even be happier after they have–no more worrying about when and if they'll ever be published. No more having to manage disappointment.

Because of course this isn't fair. Nothing in this world is. There are systemic injustices, nepotism, societal inequities that trickle into every vestige of modern life, including publishing. Being a writer takes relentlessness and determination. And three rejections is nothing. And no, your novel didn't "die on sub," you just stopped trying.

I have also listened to writers–successful writers, writers who have already accomplished more than many ever will–complain about not winning one award (when they've already won several) and about getting one rejection (when they mostly get acceptances) and about feeling insulted to the point of wishing violence upon editors for imagined or exaggerated slights.

Sigh.

I want to say:

Have some self-awareness.

Consider your audience.

Feel a bit of gratitude.

Share the wealth (and the spotlight).

Check your arrogance.

I don't, but I *do* get out of those conversations as quickly as I'm able to and with as much tact and grace as I can muster. (I will admit that after three or four "No, you're great, you can't quit, look at all your awards, no, come on, your publication record is amazings" I'm dipping out. The phone's ringing or someone's at the door or I have to take the dog out.)

Book-world-bummers come in other forms, of course, and I can't always do much about them. There will never *not* be trolls online leaving acidic comments, for one, and all I can do is unfriend them or block them or ignore them. (And remember that envy does ugly things to people.) If my work gets a negative or low-star review from a reader, I try to look at it as a rite of passage: part and parcel of what it means to be a "real" writer with published work out there for public consumption.

And when all else fails, I think of the proclamation made in the year 2000 by the all-female R&B group 3LW: "Haters gonna hate."

Now, you.

Putting space between yourself and those who would discourage you is not a one-and-done step. It's more like something you always have to be vigilant about, and deal with when and as it comes. But here are a few things to watch out for:

-Online or in-person groups that do more tearing down than building up

-Writer "friends" who come to you when they need a cheerleader but rarely ask how you're doing

-Writers who seem to be at "the top" but rant about how they've been mistreated by the industry that *put* them at the top

-Passive-aggressive comments from folks who turn on you the minute you accomplish anything

-Writers being needlessly mean about other writers on social media

Protect your inner light. I know that sounds corny, but I'm serious. That hopeful little glow inside of you that keeps you at your writing desk (and made you sit down in the first place) is precious and rare. Some people will want to snuff it out.

Don't let them.

Dare to Write in Other Genres

I used to shy away from other genres–especially poetry.

I had a prejudiced opinion of the word "poet," associating with it flakey, draining people much too caught up in gazing at their own belly buttons. (I have met poets like that–I've just learned they aren't the majority.)

Then, five or six years ago, I started dabbling. I didn't have time to write and endlessly revise a 5,000-word story, but I had time to write a poem. And the first draft of the first one (of course) wasn't very good. However, I found I had time to revise that poem...then revise it again...then a few more times. I had faculty office hours scheduled on Friday afternoons, and no college student with an ounce of self-respect was coming to talk about writing with their teacher on a Friday afternoon. So, that became my Poetry Hour.

Some of those Friday-afternoon poems got published in journals, and eventually made it into my 2023 collection, *In Memory of Exoskeletons,* like "Afternoon, 1988," "Heirloom," "Bargain," and others. And here's the thing with getting published: it feels good. It's nice. And it has a way of making a person think, "Oh, hey. Maybe I'm kinda okay at this. Maybe I *like* it."

I still don't consider myself a poet, but I concede that "I write poetry." These days, I'm still writing poetry, and it's still not exclusive. I'm a fiction writer first, but poems, like microfiction, can be great in-between-y accomplishments when I need a break from a larger project, especially if I'm feeling frustrated by it or I'm not sure how to address an issue I see. Writing a poem is like a "side quest," something I can achieve en route to a bigger goal. And because I don't have to worry about things like plot, backstory, the role of secondary characters, the protagonist's arc, etc., I can revise a poem in a reasonable time frame. And that means I have a whole, new, polished word-baby to send out into the world. It gives me a confidence boost and a bit of energy, so I can go back to my longer work-in-progress with a fresh perspective.

Another reason I recommend fiction writers play around with poetry (and micro fiction) is because in poetry, every single word counts. Not just every sentence–every word. I will *agonize* (okay not really, but almost) over the choice between "murk" and "gloom." Because they are different! Because there is no such thing as an exact synonym! Because every word carries its own shade of meaning! And *oof.* It's not just every word. It's every piece of punctuation!

Working on a granular level like that with the words that are my currency is such good training. It has broadened my vocabulary, expanding my lexicon so that I have more options when it comes to writing in any genre. It has made me think beyond the standard old comma-and-period punctuation pairing, showing me how including a colon or long dash instead can change the meaning (and reading) of a line. I've learned more about pacing and voice and tone, all because writing poetry has made me pay closer attention to the basic tools that sometimes, while writing fiction, I take for granted.

Micro fiction can do a lot of the same for you–especially if you are trying "dribbles" (50-word stories) or "drabbles" (100-word stories). Because if you come out with 52 words, or 101 words, trust me, you will analyze your language until you come up with just the write phrasing efficiency solution to make it work at 50 or 100.

So, yes. I admit it. I write poetry–and not just that. I also write the odd personal essay now and then, having recently gotten into "speculative nonfiction." My newest undertaking is a weird, braided essay about Bloody Mary–and how I'm still scared of that spooky witch. I have other essay ideas waiting for me in the wings of my brain: the Irish Potato Famine that brought my ancestors to America and the uncanny comfort I feel when my hands are in soil; the way childhood trauma led me to associate flowers with funerals until I grew them myself, grafting joy onto pain. I hope I'll have time to write them someday.

Now, you.

What genre have you been wanting to try, outside of your "home" genre?

It doesn't have to be poetry or nonfiction–it could be super short-form micro fiction, like six-word stories. Or it could be a one-act play, or a premise for a video game, or a children's picture book. It could be an interview you do with an author or publisher you admire (that you then post to your blog–*see Chapter 3—Set Up an Author Website*!). Make a word search or a crossword puzzle. Write a menu of your family's planned dinners for a week, using only ridiculously fancy words: *"Tonight's gastronomical feat will be deconstructed beef accessorized with sauteed onion and garden-fresh herbs, served aside root-vegetable reduction infused with dairy cream."* (You are eating meatloaf and mashed potatoes. Ha!)

The important thing is to get out of your comfort zone and try a new form. Have fun. You may find that you're quite good at it; you may expand your writerly repertoire. But even if not, you'll give your brain a break from some of your other projects and recognize "writer's block" for the fake news it is–when you get stuck on one story, move to an essay. Get stuck on that essay, try a poem. Sick of poetry? Go back to that story with new ideas! Then repeat. You'll never be bored, and you'll find that your "output" has increased in quantity and variety.

Plus, think of how cool your business card will be once you can add "greeting card author" and "creator of wine label descriptions," and maybe even "poet."

Consider a Writing Group

As I have mentioned in previous chapters, I am now and have been part of several writing groups, formal and informal, large and small. Not all of them have been perfect; in fact, I recount a real bummer of a workshop in *Chapter 1—Make a Start*. But, outside of a classroom, writing workshops are what the writer makes of them–especially when the writer's actually making them, and remember, that's an option: forming one instead of joining one.

For me, some of the best (and by best, I mean most helpful, most productive, most friendly, and most fun) workshops have been homemade and somewhat organic. They're the ones that formed because I or someone else said, usually via a social media direct message thread, "Hey, do you guys want to trade work for feedback?" Or, even more casual: "Can anyone read a story I want to submit on Friday?" There is no pressure, but usually someone says yes, or a couple people say yes. There's a spirit of mutual helpfulness in these tiny communities, so in the future, the asker will become the answerer, and the creative assistance goes 'round and 'round.

Another advantage to forming a feedback group with friends already in the genre is that they already "get" what I'm trying to do. They're familiar with the conventions, tropes, and subgenres, and I avoid the awkward "I don't know what this is supposed to be" comments I've sometimes gotten in non-speculative fiction groups.

However, I do love a workshop with a schedule, too, because I find those motivating. If I have a story due to my fellow writers by a certain date, I will get it to them, making sure to prioritize my writing when at other times, I may have put it off. I wouldn't be able to participate in this type of workshop every week for a whole year–not enough gas in the tank–but for three or six or 10 weeks at a time, that intensity of writing (and reviewing others' stories) brings a focus and industriousness I appreciate. (At this moment, I have about six stories written for my last workshop series waiting for me to revise them.)

I know I've said it elsewhere in this book, but horror writers can't do what they do alone. They can't write in a vacuum. They need to get others' thoughts and perspectives; they need to know what others are doing (and not doing). Plus, everything is more fun with friends, and I'm reminded of that every time I take part in a workshop.

Now, you.

If you want to try out a writing group, but you're feeling nervous about it, start small. Ask one trusted writer friend to trade work with you (and if you don't have a trusted writer friend yet, remember the recommendations from *Chapter 5—Find Your Tribe*–join an existing writers' organization, and ask for a feedback partner on your group's Facebook or Discord page). Give them quality feedback; get their quality feedback in return. You will find that it's helpful and fun. (And if it isn't, rethink that friendship!)

Next, ask a third person to join your new tiny writing group. Trade not just work, but encouragement. If you are proud of yourself for sending out a submission, tell them. Congratulate them on what they're accomplishing, even if the achievement is just finishing a first draft, or submitting a story for the first time, or getting a rejection (all important early milestones!). If you see a submission call that seems like it could be a good match for one of their stories you've reviewed, share the link.

That all sounds easy, right?

Then, when you are feeling ready for a more intense workshop experience (and if you've got a few extra bucks to spend), look for an opportunity to sign up for one. (*See Chapters 2—Get Back to Learning, 5—Find Your Tribe, and 17—Be Grateful, Not Satisfied* for more on that.)

I also have some tips to share on how to handle workshops and critiques. I learned a lot of this the hard way, but you don't have to.

-Only join or form a writing group if you genuinely want feedback and feel ready to receive it with an open mind and a positive attitude. There's no shame in not being ready for that yet, either–if your writing feels too raw or you feel too new, that's fine. Give it some time.

-Reciprocate. Ask your friend what type of feedback they want. Like, are they looking to remodel the story, or do they just want help picking a new paint color? Then, do a thorough reading of their work, making notes as you go that relate to the writer's stated needs. Keeping their feedback requests in mind will help you avoid rewriting their story for them (no one wants that!) and from leaving them proofreader marks on a first draft. (Proofreading is a last step before submission! Who cares about a misused homophone when that whole scene may change?) Don't be the workshop dud who asks for feedback without returning the favor. And if it's something like a paid-for, professionally led workshop, do your very best to keep up with the schedule.

-As an add-on to that last one, please don't waste workshop/class time arguing with the professional workshop leader. I've witnessed that, and it was cringeworthy for all of us!

-Be vocal about the kind of feedback you want when asking for help. Make a note at the top of the document and highlight it. It's up to *you* to get the most from your workshop experience, so be direct and clear with the type and level of commentary you're hoping for. (For example, you might write something like "I can't quite get the teenage protagonist's voice down. Please help!" or "I think there is a plot hole in the second half of the story–if you agree, I'd appreciate any suggestions!")

-When you do get feedback, let it sit for a few days before applying it to revisions (or disregarding it). After your initial emotional response wears off, you may change your mind about what you want to try.

-In the rare case that you end up in a workshop with a participant whose comments seem nasty, try not to take it personally. When people behave like that, it's always about them, and never about you.

-Say thank you! When (not if) you get a story from a workshop accepted for publication, thank the folks who helped you develop it. Not only is it just good manners, but it will inspire them to keep up the hard work on their own stories.

Be Grateful, Not Satisfied

Success means different things to different people.

Like many folks in this community, I had a longtime dream of becoming a "real" author, with all the quasi-official trappings: a professionally designed book cover, with my name on it, that people could buy and review. (Of course, part of that dream was that readers would *like* the book, too.)

For me, it happened in early 2023 (though the acceptance came through from Alien Buddha Press in late 2022). They wanted to publish my little collection of poetry! I got a cover from artist Chad Lutzke, and my friend Joanna helped me reserve an upscale local pub, Downtown Brew, for the launch party. That took place on March 4th, and my friends and family packed the joint; my sister Kristin even flew in from Alabama to surprise me! The horror community's very own Rocky Colavito, who was in the area visiting family, made it too. I was absolutely awash with warm fuzzies. I read a few poems (without fumbling them! I was especially nervous about the phrase "brackish woods' bracken") then signed and sold books. (Actually, my husband Joel sold books. Turns out he's a damn good bookseller.) Afterward, a bunch of us went out for tacos. All in all, it was a perfect day.

I was and still am so grateful for that entire experience.

Grateful, but not *satisfied*.

I wasn't done.

As soon as Monday rolled around, I was already plotting what my next book, or books, would be. I wrote half a novella, put it aside (figured out later it wasn't working because the protagonist is boring. *Sorry, Dani, I'll come back to you, I swear*), then wrote a whole novella. I started a novel. I *tried* to write a slasher story, but to be honest it ended up as a horror-comedy-romance. What can I say? If I put a (fictional) puddle of blood on the floor, a character's gotta slip in it, banana-peel-style. Those are, I guess, my rules.

But, being the constant student that I am, I knew it wasn't just the volume of writing that counted–it was the knowledge and the skills and the versatility that go into that writing. I wanted to learn how to write better, and in more genres and subgenres and styles. So, I applied to join Moanaria's Fright Club workshop, an intense 10-week program of writing and learning about the horror genre led by Moaner T. Lawrence. I made the cut, and school was in session. I also enrolled in additional independent studies with Lindsay Merbaum, completed a mentorship program with author Alex Seidel (I was the mentee!) through the Horror Writers Association, and participated in more workshops through *Defunkt Magazine*'s Lit Fest. I attended live-streamed talks and panels by authors I admired, like Lisa Kröger and Carmen Maria Machado.

And of course, I read my butt off.

Was it all worth it? The time, the effort, the cost of some of those workshops?

Yep. (And we'll talk financial stuff in the next chapter.)

Many of the stories and poems I wrote in and for those workshops have found homes, but more importantly, the experiences helped me become better at this thing we are all trying to do, and I got to meet some really fabulous people.

I'll always be a work-in-progress: grateful but not satisfied, wondering what else I can do. Every award nomination and publication and anthology invitation will lead to the same, echoing question: what's next?

Now, you.

Celebrate your successes–every single one.

Sometimes that means meeting a goal you set for yourself, like getting a draft done, or revising part of a story that stumped you previously, or hitting a certain word count or submission number goal. And sometimes successes will involve other, more public markers, like anthology inclusions or award nominations. Enjoy *all* of them. You deserve that.

But don't let those wins make you complacent. Because you're not done either! How can you become an even better writer? What can you write in a subgenre you haven't tackled before? What project size has intimidated you? Is there a published author's style you want to emulate (with your own flavor added, of course)?

And now we're back to the subject of finding those continuing education opportunities–looking for workshops, classes, and author talks. And if those aren't available locally or aren't within your budget, remember that lots of writing- and horror-writing-specific podcasts and blogs and YouTube videos can be accessed for free after a simple Google search.

Watch Your Spending

A big part of my trial-and-error learning in the writing world has had to do with money.

I'll tell you how I spent foolishly and how I spent wisely, but I want to preface this section with a few reminders: I'm not in this for the money, and I'm fortunate enough to have a steady job with good benefits, which means I am not in a position of having to write for my supper. Also, I'm a teacher–I don't view opportunities with cartoon dollar signs in my eyes.

Let's proceed!

Well, let's go backward, actually. To 2021, when I really started to investigate submissions opportunities and send my work out for possible publication. I was so excited, and so hopeful, that I sent work out to, like, a dozen writing contests with $25 submission fees. You read that right: I paid. Over a dozen presses. Three hundred dollars collectively. To reject my work. (Go ahead–gasp dramatically and clutch at your chest like a scandalized Victorian woman. It's the only logical response to that.)

Of course, in the heat(s) of all those moments, when I was submission drunk, getting my little dopamine hit every time I hit "send," I wasn't thinking about the annual total. I was telling myself "It's only $25! And I could win this big fancy award and a few hundred bucks! Totally worth it!" again and again. Some of those contests were for a collection–and, okay, $25 isn't ridiculous if the overall prize is a book publication. But many of those contests were single-story contests! And it was still $25 to submit!

My wake-up call came at the end of the year, when I had to add it all up. Seeing over $300 spent on submission fees alone made a little vomit rise in my throat. I tried to comfort myself, thinking "Well this is kind of a hobby. People spend money on hobbies. That's normal."

Nuh-nuh-*no*.

First, writing is my passion, not my hobby. (Wanna know the difference? Hobbies only ever make you low-level happy. Passions have enough power over your life to give you the highest of highs and, also, the lowest of lows.)

Second, spending money on a passion (or a hobby) means you are getting something: be it knowledge or experience or supplies.

I got nothing from those writing contests.

Now, I'm not a hundred percent against submission fees. I'm happy to pay something like $3, now and then, to contribute toward a publication's overhead or printing costs, or when putting a buck or two into a digital "tip jar" will get me an expedited response.

But I will never, and I mean *never*, pay $25 to submit a single flipping story to any one press, ever again. (And really, it would take quite a bit of confidence for me to pay $25 even to submit a whole collection or novel anywhere these days.)

Since January of 2022, I've cinched my purse strings a little tighter. I still spend money on writing, but only when I'll gain something: a workshop experience, a writers' retreat, knowledge, hob-nob time with author buddies and mentors (i.e. conventions). I'm also mindful of the price tags. For example, I saw a ghost story workshop advertised on social media, and it sounded so perfect for me. But when I read the fine print, I saw that two or three one-hour Zoom sessions would set me back $500. That was a no for me!

I've found plenty of free and reasonably priced events and classes, too, many of which are mentioned in other chapters, with tips for how to find them (social media searches, friends' recommendations, industry newsletters, Eventbrite.com). Overall, though, I've gotten better at asking "What's in it for me?" And if the answer is "Probably nothing," I steer clear.

Now, you.

Be smarter than 2021-me. Just say no to big submission fees, especially when the submission call is for a single story or a three-pack of poems. And when you *do* pay to submit a story or poem, don't spend more than you'd be willing to pay for a mediocre cup of coffee.

Avoid the carnival barkers. Anyone promising that their course will land you a best-seller book deal or that their workshop will guarantee you'll learn to write like Neil

Gaiman is delusional at *best*. There's no such thing as a reliable get-rich-quick scheme, and ditto for get-famous-quick schemes.

Likewise, beware predatory publishers. There are many so-called "presses" out there that charge huge fees to basically help a person self-publish. There's nothing wrong with self-publishing; there's nothing wrong with paying a fair price to take a self-publishing workshop. But if you see ads that say things like "For the low price of $5,000, we'll professionally publish your book!" then keep scrolling. (Check writerbeware.blog regularly–they try to warn writers about publishing industry scams.)

The same goes for editors. If you want to pay someone to edit your manuscript, get references and be sure of the person's competence first. Ask about their work experience, what formal education or training they have. Anyone can offer editing services for a fee, but that doesn't mean that offer is ethical. Also, research standard per-page or per-word rates for the kind of editing you need. Developmental edits, which have to do with plot and character and continuity, will cost more than line edits/copy edits. Line edits, which address the wording but not the story itself, will cost more than copy editing, and proofreading. The first reviews and corrects text for inconsistencies of style and glaring problems with grammar, spelling, and punctuation; while proofreading is the final search for spelling, punctuation, grammar, and formatting errors. Remember that professional, responsible editors shouldn't demand the whole payment in advance. (Many do require half or some of the total up front, in order to invest time into your project.) And, in most cases, you'll still want a contract first, to protect both parties. (I say "most" because I have engaged in such barters as editing-for-wine, through which I was both editor and wine-getter.)

And here's one I've only learned of more recently! I have gotten countless offers, via direct message, mostly on Instagram, by "bookstagrammers" who are willing to review my book for a fee. I'm torn on these–on one hand, it seems unethical to pay for reviews. Obviously, the review is going to be biased, and I want people to really like my book, not just pretend to because I paid them $35. On the other hand, I know from experience that reviewing books is a ton of work, and takes a lot of time. So... I dunno. Something to think about, at least. (*More on book reviews in Chapter 23—Go After Book Reviews.*)

Overall: don't spend what you don't have. Don't go into debt. And don't pin all your hopes on a promise made by someone who is making that promise to whomever will pay them the highest fee.

Find Your Way Back to Your Writing Desk

The ticking clock is the enemy of all writers. (That is why my blog is called "Writer's Block & the Ticking Clock," though I think writer's block is overblown. I just wanted the rhyme. Haha.)

We have a thousand demands calling for our attention on a weekly basis. The day job (or night job), family obligations, parenting or caretaking, chores and errands, self-care, socializing (if you're into that). So, even writers with the best of intentions and ideas coming out their ears will, sometimes, find themselves off track, realizing it's been days, or weeks, since they last wrote anything.

It happens to me now and then–especially around the winter holidays, and toward the end of every semester. My creativity feels dusty, rusty, and dry-rotted.

But it's not.

Like Jason Voorhees and his ever-evolving hockey mask, my creativity is only *temporarily* out of commission, ready to emerge from the dirty lake of disuse to slash once again.

If I'm *really* struggling to get back into my project, I do what we all do when we're in trouble: call a friend. Then make a date for a writing sprint.

Writing sprints are really helpful, in that they are dedicated, scheduled, timed intervals during which two or more buddies write together. Because, as I've said, my writer friends are cast far and wide, we do our sprints over Zoom. We get on our video call, say hello and then talk about what we're working on. Then we give it, oh, a half hour or thereabouts, shutting our cameras and microphones off but staying on the Zoom call. At the end of that interval, we turn cameras on and unmute, sharing our word counts and any relevant breakthroughs or sticking points. If we have time, we write for another half hour.

I am much more likely to make myself write if I also get friend time out of it!

Or when there is a deadline. Maybe that is a leftover motivation from my article-writing days? Or student days? I don't know. But, if I have a due date, I will get on it–like I do when I am part of an organized, official workshop, especially one I pay for (*see Chapter 16—Consider a Writing Group*).

Another trick I use when I am feeling too far gone from my writing desk is to bring my journal with me when I go to places where I know I'll have to wait–like a doctor's appointment, or the airport, or a class when my students are working independently and I'm just supervising. Usually, I'd spend those little pockets of time scrolling social media, or, as I've said, staring at my Submittable account screen, wondering when the buttons will change color. But, if I have my journal with me, I make myself use the time more wisely. If my brain feels blank, reading what's already there usually revives me enough to add some more ideas or notes or potential character dialogue.

Recently, I did not have my journal with me, and the fire alarm went off at my allergist's office. Everyone had to go outside for about a half hour (the weather was pleasant, so that was fine). I had an idea for my novel-in-progress, so I found a dirty, torn envelope in my purse, along with a pen, and got to scribbling. By the time we were allowed to go back inside, I had a new idea for a scene I'd been struggling to get right.

Something else that helps get me back to my word-nerding is being open to creative suggestion. For example, in October of 2023, poet Donny Winter posted the "Octpoember" schedule he'd created to social media. It had a different prompt listed for every day of the month, with the idea being that anyone participating could write a new poem each day or pick from the prompts on the days they had time for poetry writing. Before seeing Donny's post, I had no plans to write new poems that month. But, I ended up writing a few, and two of those qualified as revision-worthy. One of them, "It's Always a Demon," was accepted by *Dusty Attic* for publication. The other, "No Grave Marker Needed," is currently making its rounds out in the submission world. Thanks, Donny!

Now, you.

Do you have any little pockets of time in your schedule? Even five minutes of jotting down ideas is better than nothing. Maybe you take a bus to work for a commute, or have a lunch break that is usually 10 minutes of sandwich-eating and 20 minutes of boredom.

Keep a little notebook in your purse or tote or jacket pocket, so you can make use of the doctor's-office-waits and the airport-lounge-purgatory-sentences.

Or, could you do an "idea dump" right before bed? (This might help you fall asleep easier, too.) Keep a journal and pen on your nightstand, and after you snuggle in, spend five or 10 minutes writing about any poem or story ideas you have, or brainstorm about a plot hole that is stumping you, or make lists of possible character names and setting elements.

Then, when you do find yourself with a free hour or two, you can go to your notebook or journal and pluck out your most promising material to develop into something closer to a first draft!

If you have a writing buddy, whether they live near or far, see if they'd want to schedule a short writing sprint. Or, look for a submission opportunity you both like, and challenge one another to write a story/poem/essay for the call. You can trade work back and forth for feedback, keep up the revision energy, then smash that submit button before the deadline. (If you get rejected, who cares? 1. You have another tick mark for your #100rejections challenge; 2. You have a fully fledged story ready to submit to other submissions opportunities that seem fitting; and 3. You bonded with a friend over the pressure and thrill of getting in a new submission.)

Never underestimate the power of prompts. You can type "Writing Prompts" into Google and it will give you a hundred sites; or, you can just look around you. Write a story about a fictionalized version of your workplace, or create a protagonist based on the dude who rode the subway next to you that morning. Write a poem about the weather. Write a poem about the rotting leftovers in your fridge (whatever's growing the most interesting color of mold). Write an essay about the thing that still scares you at night, no matter how old you are.

You don't need anything more than what you already have to get back to writing after life has forced you to take a break. You've got your laptop or a notebook. You've got five minutes here and there, that could turn into 10 minutes, that could turn into more. And you've got that juicy, creative brain bursting with ideas that any zombie would be proud to eat.

Get back after it.

Your next story is waiting for you.

Pay It Forward

On some days–good days–I wake up full of gratitude, with a clear and crisp awareness of all I've been given: opportunities, kindnesses, friendships, support.

And on those days, I am most sure that part of my job as a writer is to do what I can for others. I may not have the fame and fortune and influence to give new writers their first breaks, but, there's still a lot I *can* give.

There are many ways to do this. Here are a few I like:

I love teaching creative writing. Even as an adjunct professor. It doesn't pay much, I know, and I get as tired of college-student excuses as any other teacher. But. I never run out of energy for my job because I will never forget how I felt when I was on their side of the classroom: that eagerness tinged with arrogance, that uncynical hope for my own writerly future. In every class, I have students who, I can tell, *want* to do this thing we do. I want to encourage them at every turn, and help them develop and broaden their writing skills with each passing week of the semester. Even after those sparkling little creatures move on to other classes, I will still be there to write them recommendation letters or be a job reference on their applications. I will be their forever cheerleader. And if that's corny, well, pass the salt and butter.

Off campus, I can pull my writer friends up when they fall into holes of self-doubt. I can tell them congratulations, sincerely, whenever they finish a draft or tackle a new project or win an award. I can like and share their posts on social media. When they publish books, I can buy copies and review them on Goodreads and post pictures of the covers to Instagram. When friends ask for book recommendations, I can share the titles of my latest favorites. And, if it's in my power to nominate their work for possible award selection, I can do that, too.

That and more.

I can tell them about submissions opportunities and (free to enter) writing contests. I can nudge them to apply for workshops I've enjoyed, I can join them for writing sprints and give them feedback on stories or poems that are mid-process.

I can be a good friend, and a good community member.

When someone is standing alone at a convention, I can say hello. I can introduce them to other folks I know–the way people did for me, in Denver in 2022. Keep the good energy going, you know?

Now, you.

When you can, offer support to other writers.

Simple, free ways to do this involve social media. Follow other writers, small presses and micro presses, reviewers and editors. Like and share their posts. Comment on their news. If they post invitations to virtual events, like readings or talks, click the "interested" button and, if you're not busy, attend. If you are able to get their books, from a retailer or the library, give them reviews on Goodreads and any other review sites you regularly visit. Even before you get a hold of their books, you can click "Want to read" on Goodreads, and that helps, too!

You know what else helps? Ask your library or local bookstore if they carry certain titles. Maybe they don't; but maybe you're not the only one who asked. Eventually, individual stores and libraries may be inspired to include more horror and small-press authors on their shelves.

If you go to conventions and get free swag, like stickers, display them somewhere people will see them, and maybe ask about them. (I pick up postcards and bookmarks and put them on the corkboard outside my office or on the students' lounge coffee tables for their perusal.) Who knows? Someone looking or asking may become a new fan!

And, overall, of course, be nice. Writing is hard. Trying to publish is harder. A little kindness can go a long way, whether you're on the giving or receiving end of that interaction.

Set Boundaries

This is a tough one. Doing this is a challenge–not just because setting boundaries in the first place takes practice and courage, but because maintaining those boundaries takes constant effort.

The peace it will bring to your life, though, is so very worth it.

I want to first clarify what boundaries are, since therapy-speak has trickled into everyday language, causing some useful concepts to lose their intended meaning. Boundaries are about the ways you allow other people to treat you–determining what behavior is acceptable, and not acceptable, in what forms and quantities. Doing this helps you to build and maintain healthy relationships with others, improves your self-esteem, and leads to more positive interactions and communication.

Boundaries can (and probably should) apply to all facets of life, but, this is a book about writing and I'm not a licensed therapist. So, I'll keep it relevant, focusing on writing time, emotional labor, and feedback requests.

Writing Time

This is precious and you must protect it at all costs. I know it sounds like I'm talking about a baby in danger of being stolen by a goblin king (*I see you, Jareth*), but it kind of is that important.

I do not always have strong willpower. I am dog-and-squirrel-style distractible. I am not always good at telling people I need space, and time, alone.

But I had to learn to be firm, with others and myself, to make sure I could sit down long enough to put words on the screen. I found that "announcements" are effective.

So, if a friend asks, say, what I'm doing on Saturday, or if I get invited to something that day, I respond with an announcement like: "Saturday is a writing day for me, but maybe another time." If I know I really need to buckle down for a day or two because a deadline is looming, I might even make that announcement more publicly, posting a similar statement to Facebook: "This weekend I will be retreating to my cave to write! See you all Monday!" And the same goes for at-home. My husband might say "Do you have to work tonight?" and I might say "Yep; gotta get a draft of this story done." Announcing what I need to do/want to do ahead of doing it lets people know that I'm not available, but it's not about them–I'm not rejecting their company, it's just that my dance card is full.

Of course, you need to know and feel that your writing time is important to be able to make those statements. If I have writing time scheduled, that is the same as a dentist appointment or RSVP confirmation. It's a valid reason to say "No, thanks" to social invitations and "Sorry, I'm not available" to favors for friends. If your friends and family members and partner and coworkers respect you, they will understand; they won't get mad. They will respond "Okay! Have fun!" or "Sounds good! Get lots of words in!" And you know what? If they *do* get mad at you for prioritizing your writing, maybe rethink the closeness of that relationship.

Emotional Labor

This is a continuation of the discussion found in Chapter 14—Dump the Negative Nellies. Emotional labor is when you change, adjust, or "edit" your feelings to benefit others and their feelings. We all do this, and it's part of caring about other people. It becomes problematic, though, when a person is doing so much of this labor that they are barely or rarely allowed to feel or talk about their own emotions–they basically get steamrolled.

Here is an example I see way too often in the writing world: Person A has gotten wonderful publication news or finished a final draft of a story they love. Their friend, Person B, is having a rough week, because they got several rejections or because they haven't been able to work out the plot holes in a story of their own. Person A calls or messages Person B to share their good news, and Person B immediately changes the conversation to how sad and disappointed they are about their situation. Person A feels bad for being excited, and guilty about their success. So Person A spends the rest of the conversation trying to cheer up Person B, therefore squashing down their happy feelings in order to emote sympathy.

(Of course, you should give your friends sympathy and understanding on their bad days, and they should do the same for you. A better version of the above conversation is to share it, 50-50, so you both feel heard. Your friends should let you talk and feel things, just like you let them talk and feel things–it's about proportion and balance.)

Another aspect of emotional labor, especially in horror writing, is more internal. We write about tough stuff. We write about death and grief and pain and fear. We do that for our characters, for our stories, and for our readers. And while we are willing to do that (or we wouldn't write in this genre), we need to be careful about sitting too long in those difficult emotions we've taken on for the sake of our stories.

I give myself what I call "palette cleansers," which are little things that tend to cheer me up or bring me joy. If I've spent the afternoon writing a really sad story (I write a lot of grief horror), I will go outside to spend time in the garden afterward (yay for fresh air and green, growing things!) or watch a funny movie with my husband, or spend time with my ridiculous orange cat, Barnaby, who has not spent one moment of his life being sad. When I lay down my pen (stop typing), I lay down those feelings.

Feedback Requests

I manage feedback requests from writer friends and from my college students–past and present. Sometimes I get overwhelmed by them. Sometimes I overpromise and underdeliver. Cards on the table: I'm still working on this.

I want to give my friends feedback. Really and truly. I love reading their work, and the act of doing that and giving them feedback teaches me things and makes me a better writer. It's also wonderful to see the writers around me growing and developing story to story. And I'm happy to give them feedback for reasons of self-interest–I give feedback to them and I ask for their feedback in return. It should be a win-win.

But, like emotional labor, there needs to be balance, and I get it wrong sometimes. I've said I'd read someone's novel draft, not recognizing I couldn't do that on any kind of timeline. I've said yes to three graduating seniors asking me to review their grad school writing samples, in the same week. I've given deep and detailed feedback to a friend a dozen times only for them to read one or two stories and give me almost no notes.

And all of those things ended up causing me stress and guilt and resentment.

More recently, I've tried to be more careful with what I promise and when. I prioritize feedback for friends who do the same for me. I'm honest when I can't get to something any time soon. Sometimes, I ask a friend to ask me again the next week, like "I have such a busy week this week, and I don't want to forget about it. If it can wait until next week, can you ask me again then?" If they don't have a deadline, they are okay with that; if they do have a deadline, they understand and ask someone else. (It's harder to manage student requests, because I feel obligated as an employee and as a mentor. But I'm working on keeping those manageable, too.)

I am not so in-demand when it comes to blurb requests, but many writers are, and I have seen evidence of them figuring out this balance, too. I've seen posts on social media like "I won't be taking any more blurb requests for the next six months, as I have several to do. Thank you for understanding!" The same goes for book reviewers–they make public announcements when their to-read lists are just too long to take on any more. (As a current asker-for-blurbs, I keep this in mind and always understand if someone says no, or not right now.)

Now, you

How do the people in your life, likely unknowingly, impede your writing time or distract you from it? What are friends and coworkers asking you or asking of you? Do they respect you as a writer, and do they consider this endeavor to be worthy and central to your life? (And, for those budding writers whose ambitions are still private, I suggest protecting your writing time by folding it into your schedule in other ways–instead of setting aside an hour three times a week at home, maybe you spend your lunch breaks writing, or go to the library for a couple hours on a Saturday to combine the trip with finding new reading materials. I can't advocate for outright lying about how you spend your time though–no one wants to be accused of infidelity when they are just hanging out with the fictional people in their head! And hey–maybe now's the time to tell your loved ones what you're up to. They might be way more supportive than you predicted.)

Answer those questions honestly, and then think about what you can do to improve those aspects of your relationships.

Sometimes, a solution is easy: Your coworker Margo invites you to the baby shower of a colleague you barely know. You've already contributed $5 to the gift fund. So you reply "Thanks so much for including me, Margo, but Saturday is a writing day for me. I hope you all have a great time, and congrats again to Laura!" What Margo thinks about your reply is irrelevant; you've been polite and assertive and wished everyone well.

Sometimes a solution is not easy, and compromises have to be made between writing and the other important obligations in your life. Like parenting. Because it's not fair to expect your co-parent to do all the chores, every night, so you can get two hours of uninterrupted writing time after work.

Create an acceptable trade. What does your partner enjoy doing that would be easier for them to do without your little darlings vying for their attention? Could you give them a game night each week with their friends, and ask for a writing night in return? Do they want the house to themselves for an afternoon, when you could take the kids to the playground or ferry them to their various activities? Ask them what they enjoy and what they wish they had more time for. (And there's an added bonus to this: when each person has their own interests and activities, there's more to talk about when you are together.)

On to emotional labor. If you find that you have friends who ask more of you than you do of them, all the time, or who steamroll all of your feelings in favor of theirs, back away from those relationships! Or, if you value them but need a change in order to continue the friendship, try being direct. Send them a message or email: "Hi Tara, I really appreciate having you in my life, but it seems like every time we talk, you don't care about what's going on with me. The conversation is always about you and your feelings, and it makes me feel like I don't matter to you–like you don't value our friendship, beyond having me as a sympathetic ear." The way they respond is going to tell you all you need to know about whether or not your relationship can be salvaged.

(Oh–and if, in reading this, you realize YOU are the friend who is always steamrolling others' feelings, well, there's no time like the present to work on being a better friend. This kind of check-in is always good for us.)

And when it comes to giving others feedback, fight your people-pleasing tendencies. One thing that can help is delaying your response in order to consider your schedule and your own to-do list. You do not have to be sneaky about this. A simple "Oh, your story sounds great! Of course, I would like to help, but can I get back to you tomorrow? I just want to check to make sure that I have the time. Don't want to promise something and then let you down!"

If you do make a promise or an agreement that you fall down on, be honest and apologize: "I'm sorry I couldn't get you feedback in time. I really wanted to, but I should have been more realistic about the time I had." (I had to do this recently.) The writer may be disappointed, but they will (hopefully) appreciate the sentiment, and the fact that you reached out.

We all want to do the best we possibly can for our loved ones and community members. But creating boundaries and doing our best to keep them intact will ensure our own needs and priorities aren't squeezed out by the needs of others.

Collaborate With Editors

Editors aren't the enemy.

Editors are the saviors, the problem solvers, the safety nets, the voices of reason, and the bringers of consistency. They are the strings tethering writers to the earth, making sure we don't float away and get lost in the liminal spaces between reality and imagination.

In short: we need them, and we need to learn to work with them, not against them.

I speak from experience on both sides of the page. Editing for a small press gave me a lot of insight into that relationship, and I quickly learned what it took to make that relationship a good one–or a troubled one.

Some authors were a teamwork dream. They understood where I was coming from when I made a comment or a suggestion (and I always made sure to explain). They wanted their books to shine as brightly as possible, and either made the changes I suggested or worked with me to find a compromise or a new solution neither of us had thought of previously. When they didn't want to change something I'd marked, they told me why. The result of all that was a better and more professionally produced book, every time.

Then there were not-so-great-to-work-with authors. Authors who argued snarkily in the comments section rather than working to find feasible solutions. Authors who stubbornly clung to passages or sections or character aspects or plot turns that just didn't work. And, well, friends, that is a quick way to ensure that editors don't want to see your names come across their desks ever again. Not good. Remember, especially within one genre, word travels fast among publishers. Do you really want to be known as the writer who throws temper tantrums, who can't play nice with others?

No.

So I keep this in mind as an author, and I pick my battles.

Most of the time, when editors have wanted to make changes to my work (post-acceptance, pre-publication), I say yes with no regrets. They want a line to read more clearly, or they want to change the pacing slightly, or they think one word would sound better than another. I am happy with all that–it doesn't change the content and doesn't affect the essence of what I created.

Other times, I've said yes to editors' changes even though I haven't *loved* them. Why? Because of gratitude and respect, and because I understand that published work isn't mine alone: it's ours. Mine and the editor's, mine and the publisher's. We create the product together. And unless I am self-publishing–a route I may go in the future when I know more about the business aspect of publication–I don't get to make every single decision. (For the record, I haven't approved any changes I've hated.)

The few times I've pushed back on something, I've done it with kindness and with an explanation, telling the editors why I want something to remain as-is, leaving any sass out of my tone. So far, every time I have done so, the editor has been fine with it–perhaps because, in general, I don't make their jobs harder.

When editors want to publish my work *and* make it better, my only response is "Please and thank you."

Now, you

Keeping your ego in check goes a long way toward fostering successful relationships with editors. Your opinion is your opinion; your mind, beautiful and complex as it is, is just one mind. Everyone benefits from collaboration.

To put that into practice:

Do not respond immediately to emails containing edits. There is no need to message back right away with a "Sure, whatever you want!" or a "Hands off my story!" If you feel like you have to acknowledge the email, keep it short: "Thanks for sending these! I'll look them over and get back to you soon."

Then, read the edits. Still, do not respond. Go do something else: wash the dishes, walk the dog, get some words down for your current WIP. Hours later, or even the next day, go back to the edits. Go through and approve all the ones that are easier to approve, and then think about the rest. Can you see how the edit is beneficial? Does it make the story or poem or essay better? Even if you liked the way you had it, do you like this, too?

If the answer is yes, approve it. If the answer is no, politely say why, and maybe suggest another potential fix.

After you've gone through the document, go through it *again*, reconsidering your responses. *Then* send it, with a polite note thanking the editor for all of their time, and asking if they can review your notes at their convenience.

When they write back, do it all over again, until you get a finished product that makes you both happy. And remember to thank them again!

Go After Book Reviews

This is one of those key pieces to being a writer that I'm still figuring out, but I can share what has and hasn't worked for me, and the ways in which I'm still experimenting.

My first book came out in March of 2023, and the publisher uses Kindle Direct Publishing (print on demand, or POD), as many small and micro presses do. It's just too expensive for them to print, ship, and store books like the huge publishing companies can.

The advantages of POD include affordability for both the publisher and the buyer, quick shipping, and–very important–the chance to make changes to the text or cover whenever necessary. For example, if a book wins an award, the publisher can add that to the cover and all books sold afterward will have the updated version. Or, if the publisher or author notices a mistake–a misspelling, formatting weirdness, etc.–that can be fixed, too. (But if you print a mistake in 500 copies, well, that mistake stays in 500 copies!)

The disadvantage of print-on-demand publishing is that the book will not be sold in most brick-and-mortar bookstores, and *that* means it's not getting the passerby exposure that many authors hope for.

Additionally, if a small press can't afford a subscription to Edelweiss or a similar online platform (where booksellers can post new releases in advance of publication to encourage preorders and reviews), it's harder to generate early buzz.

So, authors like me have to try other publicity strategies, and that's tough–not only because it may be uncomfortable to self-promote, but because it takes time and knowledge of industries most people don't have. I'm chasing a Public Relations degree, but I don't know a lot about marketing or advertising. I'm not a graphic designer. But I have to try to do a lot of those things to get my book out in the world.

One step I've taken and will continue to take, of course, is to ask readers to post a review of my book. But I can't apply too much pressure, and it's not a good idea to nag folks about it. To encourage reviews of *In Memory of Exoskeletons*, I've announced that anyone who posts a review will be entered in a raffle to win a free copy of my 2024 hybrid collection from Alien Buddha Press, *Self-Made Monsters*. That has earned me a few more reviews, but like I said: this is a hill I'm still climbing.

(Which is not to say readers haven't shown up for me. One recent review on Goodreads hit me hard in the feels on a bad day: "I love this collection. This is my first book of Rebecca's poetry and I wasn't disappointed. The title poem is one of my faves with its super-relatable deep dive that ends so subtly as if it never got wet." Thank you, Casey Kiser, you beautiful human. You will never know what that meant to me.)

Another way I have been able to get a few reviews is by looking up book reviewers on various social media platforms and messaging them directly to see if they'd consider reviewing my book. I offer to send them a free copy in exchange, though I know this is still asking them to do a great deal of work: read my book, organize their thoughts, put them in writing, post them to their own websites and platforms. Finding those reviewers takes time, as does sorting book reviewers from pay-to-play book advertisers (who also call themselves reviewers).

This is a sticking point for me and many people. On one hand, yes, reviewing a book takes so much time and effort. It's work. So why shouldn't "influencers" be paid for their labor? On the other hand, a book review that the author pays for isn't going to be objective–as I said, it's more of an advertisement than a review. I would not judge another author for going this route, and who knows, I may do this in the future, though I've chosen not to so far.

The reviewers who have not charged me for their reviews have been lovely people. They have their own review channels on YouTube, or accounts across social media platforms, and they offer honest reviews to their followers as a form of content creation. I will continue to look for these folks as I can, and when I get a "yes," I'll link their reviews to my website and share them on my own social media accounts to help promote those reviewers' brands, accounts, and channels.

Now, you

This is how I operate, and it's how I hope you will, too. Be honest and kind and supportive of other authors. Put up reviews on Goodreads and Amazon. What goes around will come around, eventually, and you can't ask of others what you're unwilling to do yourself.

If you publish your own books or go with a micro press that doesn't have a marketing budget, you will have to seek out reviews on your own.

Try the usual: ask your readers, (who are also oftentimes your friends), to post reviews on Goodreads and Amazon, as well as on their social media accounts, if they are willing. Consider offering a raffle of some kind–with a free book or some swag, like stickers and t-shirts, to send the winner.

Then hit the ol' search button on whichever social media platforms you use, and search for "book reviews." Try the words alone and as a hashtag: "#bookreviews." Message the folks who look legit, but remember, you will encounter a lot of book advertisers who want to be paid. (Recently, I had one message me directly to offer me a retweet for 20 bucks. Sir, you better be pretty darn famous for me to part with a twenty for you to hit one button. The thrift store pants I'm wearing RIGHT NOW cost $4.99.) But, even when declining those offers, be polite: "Thanks so much, but that's not in my budget right now. All the best to you!" (Because I truly believe in witchcraft's Power of Three: what you put out into the world will revisit you threefold. You don't want that to be nastiness or flippancy.)

If you have a digital copy of your manuscript ready pre-publication, even if you do self-publish, you can always offer it to readers yourself in exchange for honest reviews. No promises here–I've gotten crickets at times with that offer–but it's worth a shot.

All we can do is try, and keep trying, and when we fail, try again.

That's my plan, anyway.

Join me?

Move Forward

Ever onward.

Adjust and readjust your goals to fit your lifestyle. Do what you can, when you can. Learn and grow and *write, write, write*, letting yourself and your talent evolve.

And if you are lucky, if you do it right, you will never be done.

One of my writing students asked me a question at the end of a fall semester. She said, "How do you know when your writing is good enough? How do you know that you're good enough at writing?" And I laughed, because my answer made me happy: Never.

Writers who love writing won't run out of stories to tell. They won't ever look at a second draft and say "Eh, good enough." They won't be content writing the same three stories again and again. They will want to try new things, write in new genres, challenge themselves, give their readers a surprise. They want to expand their repertoire. They want to have fun.

And the breadth of what is possible does not just cover what they can write now or in the future; it spans technology and content consumption.

When I was a kid in the 80s and 90s, there weren't that many huge-name authors. Why? Because of gatekeeping. Everything was printed and snail-mailed. Authors always needed agents, and there weren't too many small or micro presses to get excited about indie authors and new writers.

But the internet changed all of that.

Soon, desktop publishing and online readers opened the market to just about everyone. Independent presses popped up like mushrooms on wet shag carpet. Authors could invest in basic software and publish their own books. No marketing budget? That was a bigger obstacle before social media existed to help spread the word. With the internet, venues opened up. We got online magazines and journals, blogs, subscriber accounts like Patreon and Substack. We got YouTube, which is full of shows featuring authors and their work. Podcasts became a thing! And not just news podcasts, but story podcasts, like *Creepy* A Horror Podcast with Jon Grilz and *Terrify Me! with Anthony Frost* and a few dozen others.

In short, the internet crashed the gate(keepers). Sure, agents and traditional publishing still exist, but they aren't the only options anymore. The result is more opportunities for more writers, more diversity in who gets published, and many different avenues to reach readers.

So, yeah, maybe a writer has been published in a magazine, but not an anthology. Or in an anthology, but not on a podcast. Or on a podcast, but not on a YouTube show. You get the point. The writing world and all of its possibilities are vast; each writer's potential and ability to create are vast. There is no limit; there is no *done.*

But, despite personal growth and measures of success, sooner or later we all meet a demon called Imposter Syndrome.

Imposter Syndrome is the feeling that you don't belong, or you don't deserve your success. The fear that at any moment, someone will unmask you for the fraud you think you are.

But, hoo boy, does my buddy James Sabata (horror author, screenwriter, editor, co-host of TheNecronomi.Com, and founder of Spirited Giving) have a story for you. He's agreed to let me include it (thanks, James!).

Here it is:

"In 2014, I worked in Guest Relations at Phoenix ComiCon, and one of the celebrities in my care was Stan Lee, one of the most prolific creators in comics, having co-created Spider-Man, the Avengers, The X-Men, and so many more. There isn't a person alive who loves comics who wasn't influenced by Stan Lee in some way. I was excited to get Stan on my list, but I had no idea how much a single conversation would influence the rest of my life.

"It was late Friday evening when Stan asked to take me and a few of the other staff working with him to a bar and loudly announced he was paying. I thanked him but told him I do not drink. He smiled broadly and bellowed, 'Then we got ourselves a safe driver to get us back!'

"He ordered everyone refills throughout the night and I watched as he took joy in getting everyone a little too intoxicated. He told us stories, made jokes, and occasionally gave us pieces of advice. He was speaking to me and another writer and asked us if we still experienced Imposter Syndrome. We, of course, said we do and Stan laughed, 'Oh, good! It's not just me!' And then STAN F'N LEE told us how every single morning for most of his life, he's expected someone to show up and say, 'How did you get all of this? You're not good enough to do this! You're a phony!' I'll never forget the mix of guilt and disgust on his face with the word 'phony.'

"But it rocked my world just the same. That was the day I gave up on Imposter Syndrome. Not that I don't experience it, but I no longer let it stand in my way. You shouldn't either. I think about it often. I share this story anytime I can. If the great Stan Lee, at 90 years of age, was still plagued by the occasional flare of Imposter Syndrome, I assume there's not a lot of hope for any of us ever fully defeating it. And you know what? That's okay.

"We don't have to destroy it. It's enough to accept that it's not going anywhere; maybe learn to live with it. Once we do, we are free to move forward. Imposter Syndrome can follow along, but don't let it stand in the way.

"As Stan always said, 'Excelsior!'"

Now, you

Jump in. Do it. Do it all and then some. Do it all so hard and so well that you eventually write your own book about how you did it.

Come to cons. Say hello, meet people, and hug the folks who are cool with hugs (gotta ask first!). Write your ass off. Get your ass back, then *submit* your ass off. Haunt those editors until you become a household name. Never give up on getting into your dream pub. Don't let the word "hard" turn into "impossible." Learn from the writers and teachers around you. Take advantage of every opportunity you can. Add "yet" to "haven't" and mean it.

In closing, let me introduce you to a fabulous new horror writer who's gonna shake the world harder than a passel of hungry Graboids.

Look in the mirror and smile,

because friend,

it's

you.

About the Author

Rebecca Cuthbert is a dark fiction and poetry writer. She loves folklore, witchy women, and anything that involves nature getting revenge. Her debut poetry collection, *In Memory of Exoskeletons*, is available through Alien Buddha Press. Additional titles are scheduled for release in 2024 and 2025, including the hybrid collection *Self-Made Monsters* (ABP, Oct. 2024).

Rebecca's stories and poems can be found in *Shakespeare Unleashed* (Monstrous Books and Crystal Lake Publishing), *We're Here: The Best Queer Speculative Fiction 2022* (Neon Hemlock Press), *Dread* (Cemetery Dance Publications), *Soul Scream Antholozine* (Seamus & Nunzio Productions), and in other magazines and anthologies.

She serves as the editor-in-chief of PsychoToxin PINK, the feminist horror imprint of PsychoToxin Press, and teaches creative writing classes at SUNY Fredonia.

Rebecca lives in Western New York with her husband Joel, their menagerie of pets, and a garden full of demanding plants.

Visit rebeccacuthbert.com for publications, events, news, and more.

ACKNOWLEDGEMENTS

Usually, writers and editors have to agonize over manuscripts for months or years before they see their book in print.

But, from the word go, that wasn't the case for me and Christopher Ryan, editor-in-chief and publisher of Seamus & Nunzio Productions.

He emailed me early in the fall of 2023 and asked if I wanted to write a book–he explained the premise, and the purpose, and his vision for the finished product. Was I in? Hell yes I was.

Like a fast-spreading zombie apocalypse, the book took on a life of its own, growing by the day. The chapters (almost) wrote themselves–"Be yourself," Chris told me. "Tell your story." So I did. And by January of 2024, we had ourselves a book.

There are so many people to thank for CREEP's existence (Yep, Chris and I have a pet name for our book), but he's who I need to start with. This book was Chris's brainchild–he brought me in to help make it a reality. He's an incredibly supportive editor, smart with suggested changes and willing to negotiate for workable solutions. If you are a writer and get a chance to work with him, do it. Thank you, Chris. I'm lucky to count you as an editor, publisher, and friend.

Next I would like to thank my husband, Joel, whose patience with me over months of almost full-time writing borders on the epic. I couldn't have accomplished any of it without his encouragement, love, and sense of humor. Thanks, honey. I'm so fortunate to have you.

There are no terms good enough to thank the horror community and all of the people in it who have shown me kindness, given me friendship, and offered me encouragement, but I'll try. You all provided me and my work with a home. You welcomed me into your world when you didn't have to. You invited me to your workshop groups, to your social media pages, and even to a few anthologies and podcasts. You made me feel like I belong. Thank you.

Special thanks to the Horror Writers Association, which proved to be the gateway to where I am now. Thank you to HWA-NY, whose members welcomed this Buffalo gal. Thank you to Lindsay Merbaum and The Coven. Thank you to Moaner T. Lawrence and Fright Club. To Jensen Sikora for their artwork and generosity. Thank you to my Wednesday Workshop friends, especially Alexis DuBon, Rae Knowles, and Rowan Hill. Thank you to all my #100rejections buddies and my Discord group comrades. Thank you to Lisa Kröger and Melanie R. Anderson. Thank you to Jonathan Gensler, Kevin Kennel, James Sabata, S.A. Bradley, Bridget D. Brave, P.L. McMillan, Angela Sylvaine, Don Guillory, Rocky Colavito, Joshua Gage, Alex Simmons, Brian Keene, Laurel Hightower, D.M. Guay, Anton Cancre, Jason McCord, Sofia Ajram, Chris O'Halloran, T.J. Price, Robert Perez, and Joseph Wilson. Thanks to Red Mitchell at Alien Buddha Press, Hannah Kludy and Morgan Wagle and the gang at *Nocturne Horror Magazine*, Diamond Braxton and the *Defunkt Magazine* crew, Kimberly Glanzman and everyone at *Miniskirt Magazine*, Josh Darling and Jacque Day at *Carnage House*. Thank you James Chambers, Carol Gyzander, Christopher Pelton, Roxie Voorhees, Kevin Lucia, James Aquilone, Chad Lutzke, J.G. Faherty, Ruth Anna Evans, Vincent V. Cava, Jared Sage, Tim McGregor, John Collins Jr., Robert P. Ottone. Thanks to every editor and publisher who has given my work a chance to find its readers, to every reader who has spent their precious time reading my stories and poems, to reviewers who read and wrote about my work, and to the online and in-person audiences who have attended or listened to my readings.

To the folks in my life who tolerate and even endorse my weirdness: thank you. Thanks to writing buddies Heather Frese-Sanchez, Kelly Sundberg, Keema Waterfield, and Sara Lucas. To my Watson (S.E. Reichert). To N. West Moss. To Sarah Gerkensmeyer. To Joanna Kaufmann. Thanks to my students for being proud of me, to my colleagues for cheering me on. To my closest friends who know that writing is one of only three topics I can converse on and being okay with it (the others are dogs and gardening). To my family, Schwab side and Cuthbert side, for being excited about my projects for me and with me. To my community at Lakeshore Humane Society.

This list is ridiculous, and it's still too short–I could add 50 more names. All of this is because of all of you. And I am so very grateful.

Also by Rebecca Cuthbert

Also by Seamus and Nunzio Productions

Here's a gallery of Seamus and Nunzio Productions projects:

SOULSCREAM Antholozine

Original Novels:

Coming in 2024

Made in United States
Orlando, FL
24 January 2024